CW00972307

TIBET

The Jesuit Century

PHILIP CARAMAN

HALSGROVE

First British edition published in 1998 by Halsgrove
Copyright © 1997 Philip Caraman

ISBN 1 874448 73 6

British Library Cataloguing-in-Publication-Data
CIP data for this book is available from the British Library

HALSGROVE
Halsgrove House
Lower Moor Way
Tiverton
Devon EX16 6SS
01884 243242
01884 243325
http://www.halsgrove.com

Printed and bound in Great Britain
by Bookcraft Ltd, Midsomer Norton

Contents

Illustrations

1. Bento de Goes
   An idealized portrait from a painting in the Jesuit College of Tortosa, reproduced in Matteo Ricci, *Opere storiche*, ed. P. Tacchi Venturi (Macerata, 1911–13)
2. Matteo Ricci (left)
   Frontispiece to vol.I of *Opere Storiche*.
3. Lhasa and the Potala*
4. Tibetan hermit (nineteenth century)†
5. Adam Schall*
6. The Kalmak Tartar tribe in the region of Lake Koko-Nor* as described by Grueber to Athanasius Kircher. Fig. I (right), Kalmak lama in red hat, yellow tunic and white cloak. Fig. II (left), Kalmak man in leather suit and yellow cap. Fig. III (centre), Kalmak woman in leather suit dyed either yellow or red. The lama has a prayer wheel by his right leg, the first drawing of the wheel in the West.
7. Travel in the Himalayas I (nineteenth century)†
8. Travel in the Himalayas II (nineteenth century)†

*Sketches by Johannes Grueber, in Athanasius Kircher, *China Illustrata* (Amsterdam, 1667)
†Reproduced in Régis-Evariste Huc, *Travels in Tartary, Tibet, and China during the Years 1844–1846* (London, 1856)

iv

Acknowledgements

My principal debt is to Edmund Ryden, S.J., of the University of Fujen, Taiwan, for the help he gave me as I was writing this book. An indication of the extent of this assistance is our correspondence over a long period. Mr Phil Weare of Taunton has taken great pains over the maps of a country largely unknown at the time of the Jesuit travellers. Sir Allan Ramsay has been my monitor in writing of the Muslims and has done me the kindness of reading the final typescript with great care. In Rome I have received every courtesy from the staff of the central Jesuit Archives and from the librarians of the Jesuit Historical Institute. I should also thank David Brigstocke, Bernard Hall, Max Rothwell, and Ignatius St Lawrence, who have helped me in a variety of ways.

Background

Herodotus, the Greek historian of the fifth century B.C., mentions India but says nothing of the massive mountains in the north of the subcontinent. There is nothing in his writings suggesting that he had any knowledge of Tibet, though he has a curious story of gold-digging ants. This was an ancient legend originating far north of Tibet in the Altai Mountains of western Mongolia: it was due no doubt to the way all the great rivers flowing from the Himalayan Range brought down with their sand grains of gold, depositing them not only in India, but in Burma and in the Yangste, the Yellow River and in China.

Three hundred years after Herodotus, Alexander the Great, having conquered the Persians in 333 B.C., twice crossed the Hindu-Kush Range and learned of the Himalayas, which he called the Emodus Mountains; and he rightly placed there the source of the River Indus. Neither Alexander nor any of his generals, however, knew anything of a country further to the north.

In A.D. 21 another Greek, Strabo, a geographer, historian and philosopher, collected in his *Geographia* the total knowledge of the world of his day: the information that the work contains about people, countries and places he derived from his reading and from his own travels in North Africa, Europe, and western Asia. But in his exhaustive compendium there is no mention of Tibet, nor is there any indication that the country was even mistily known to his world.

In the next century another geographer, namely Ptolemy (who was also an astronomer and whose writings became the standard textbook throughout the Middle Ages), had a clearer idea of where the great rivers of India rose, but still knew nothing of Tibet: the country was so unknown then and throughout the early Middle Ages that no space was left for it on contemporary maps of the world. The Arabs about the twelfth century were the first to hear of Tibet, but they had no idea where to place it on Ptolemy's map. Even to this day the antiquity of the country remains a mystery and, with the exception of the region bordering on China, nothing is known of its inhabitants before the seventh century.

1

It was through the Chinese that any reliable and partially detailed information on Tibet filtered into Europe. When the country was unknown in the West, the Chinese had a clear concept of its geography, especially its western and southern areas, but were not interested in the more remote cold, uninhabited regions that were as unknown to them as to the rest of the world.

It was left to the Franciscan and Dominican friars in the thirteenth century to bring back from their journeys to Mongolia, China and the distant areas of Asia the first somewhat piecemeal information on Tibet. At the Ecumenical Council of Lyons in 1245, Pope Innocent IV proclaimed a crusade to halt the Mongol advance that threatened the devastation of western Europe. But he first sent a Franciscan friar, John de Plano Carpini, as his special envoy to the Grand Khan to negotiate a peace: the right wing of the Mongol army had already captured and destroyed Kiev and had passed through Poland, while the main body had entered Hungary and won a great victory at Buda.

Setting out from Lyons for the unknown East, Friar Carpini, a man of sixty-five, carried with him letters from Innocent IV to Kuyuk Khan, whose court at the time was near the city of Karakorum, now a ruin in central Mongolia. Kuyuk Khan replied by threatening the Pope with further destruction. Carpini's mission had failed, but he returned with the first report to reach western Europe of a country called Tibet: he had heard of it from the Chinese, whose geographical position, commercial interests, politics, and perhaps most of all, Buddhist zeal interested them in all parts of central Asia.

Carpini had been told of the strange customs of the people who lived there beyond the frontiers of China: how when a man's father died they ate his flesh, an embroidered tale of their procedure of carving up their dead and leaving the portions to be consumed by vultures and wild beasts. The friar reported also that these men had no beards and went around carrying an iron instrument with which they plucked out at once any hairs that might happen to grow on their chins.

Setting out on a different and purely religious mission from Acre in 1252, another Franciscan, William of Rubruck, a Fleming, returned to Europe three years later after a journey of one thousand miles: he brought back reports about the Tangut, a people of northern Tibet bordering on western China: they were very brave, strong, tall, and swarthy; there was gold easily dug up in their country and beasts of burden not known in Europe, the yaks, like

> very strong oxen with tails all hair like horses, and hairy bellies and backs; they are shorter in the legs than other oxen but very much stronger. . . . The cow will not let herself be milked unless it is sung to: they are of the same nature as bulls, for if they see a man wearing red they rush upon him and would kill him.

William also spoke of the gold found in the country, and the way the people made fine goblets from their parents' skulls in order to be mindful of them during their carousals.

But like Friar John, William of Rubruck obtained his information from others and had little notion of the geographical position of Tibet. He was a missionary and in no sense an explorer. It was left to the Venetian Marco Polo to discover the country.

The pioneer of Asiatic exploration, Marco Polo visited the court of Kublai Khan, the grandson of the conqueror Ghengis Khan, in 1275, just eight years after he had transferred his court from Karakorum to Peking.The narrative of Marco Polo's journey contains the most reliable information about Tibet to reach Europe in the Middle Ages. The Venetian speaks of both a people and a country called Tebet. 'They go about filthy and begrimed,' he wrote, reflecting the prejudice of the Chinese from whom he obtained his information,

> devoid as they are of respect for themselves or for those who see them; they keep the dirt on their faces, never wash or comb, but always remain in a state of squalour. These people also have the custom . . . that if a man is condemned to death and executed by the lawful authority, they take his body, cook it and eat it. But if anyone dies a natural death, then they will not eat the body.

Marco Polo visited only the borderlands of Tibet that were subject to the Great Khan but never entered Tibet proper. He had gathered his information from travellers on the trade routes between western China and Tibet and was the first to gain some idea of the extent of the country. He had heard that it was so great that it embraced eight kingdoms and contained rivers and lakes in which gold dust was found. In one place he says that the country contained a vast number of cities and villages, but he also speaks of vast empty spaces through which a man can ride without finding any inhabitants whatever.

This is all hearsay, in some places exaggerated, in others accurate. For instance, he writes of mastiff dogs as big as donkeys that were admirable for attacking wild beasts and particularly wild oxen, for he was told that the people lived by the chase as well as by their cattle and the fruits of the earth. He narrates that they had none of the Great Khan's paper money but instead used salt, and that they had a language of their own which like the country and the people they called Tebet.

Marco Polo had approached closer to the country than either John de Carpini or William of Rubruck and had spoken with natives on the trade route from western China. Since it is claimed for him that 'he came in a brief space to know several languages and four sundry written characters', he may well have learned a smattering of Tibetan, for he uses an occasional Tibetan word like *beyamini* for wild oxen and *gudderi* for musk.

However Marco Polo knew nothing of southern Tibet. He has no reference to the Himalayas or to the great rivers. Surprisingly, he had heard nothing of Lhasa, which traded with China; he is unjust in his opinion of the inhabitants, whom the Jesuits were to find the most kind-hearted, hospitable and gentle-tempered people of central Asia. When he writes that they considered it no sin to rob and maltreat others, he is no doubt referring to the brigands north of the inland sea of Koko-Nor, who lived by attacking caravans on the road to Lhasa and are described in detail by the Abbé Huc in the account of his journey to the Tibetan capital in the mid-nineteenth century.

Marco Polo returned to Venice in 1295. The first European to have visited Tibet was Friar Oderic de Pordenone, who entered the country from China in 1330; Oderic never crossed Tibet proper and gives only a jejune account of the country. He speaks of its capital Gota (Lhasa), the first Westerner to mention it, but there is no evidence that he ever visited the city.

During the next three hundred years Tibet was forgotten. In spite of Marco Polo and the friars, the country remained unmarked on the maps. Whatever was written about Asia did nothing more than repeat Ptolemy. The great rivers, the Satlej, the Ganges, and the Indus, were better known to the ancient Romans than to the geographers of the sixteenth century. The Himalayas were still thought to separate India from Tartary and Scythia. No European had penetrated beyond the high mountain ranges to the north of India. Tibet was somewhere there to be rediscovered.

Before the end of the sixteenth century, Akbar, the great Mogul Emperor of India, had succeeded in enlarging his dominions to include Afghanistan, Baluchistan, and all India north of the River Godavari. For the defence of his vast empire, he initiated an investigation into the countries on both sides of his northern frontier and published the findings of his commission in a work entitled *Ain-Abari*. It is full of fascinating information about India; but though his commissioners knew about Kashmir, they equated Tibet with Baltistan. The report noted that 'gold is imported into Hindustan and is to be found in abundance in the northern mountains of the country as well as in Tibet.' Marco Polo, now long forgotten, had been more informative on Tibetan gold than Akbar's commissioners. 'These people,' he had written about the Tibetans, 'have much gold in their country, so that when a man lacks gold he digs till he finds it and takes only as much as he requires and puts the rest back in the ground; for if he put it in his treasury or coffer he maintains that God will take away from him that which is in the ground.' This gold, first mentioned by Herodotus, was found in the form of nuggets as well as in spangles and dust: the nuggets were carefully replaced or left intact by the Tibetans in the belief that they were live organisms and produced spangles and dust which would otherwise disappear if they were removed.

But it would seem that though Akbar knew of a country called Tibet, he knew nothing of its location. He was told that 'a class of lamas or Mongolian devotees', existed there, 'recluses and hermits who lived for two hundred years and more'. But where these people lived and where they should be located on the map was still unknown. In fact, sixteenth-century knowledge of Tibet was still nebulous in comparison with that of the medieval friars whose information was drawn principally from Chinese sources.

However, the Jesuits and Emperor Akbar both had their own motives for journeying into these unmapped and unknown regions beyond the northern boundaries of the Empire. Akbar was anxious to secure his northern frontiers, the Jesuits were in search of the Christian communities rumoured to exist somewhere in central Asia in a country known to Marco Polo as Cathay.

In October 1602 Bento de Goes, a Portuguese Jesuit Brother who had won the confidence of Akbar, set out from Agra with the Emperor's benediction, travelled to Kabul, crossed the Hindu Kush and the southern Gobi Desert, and three years after setting out reached Su-cheu in western China; there he died in April 1607. On his epic journey he had filled in gaps on the map of central Asia but had gathered no information on Tibet, for he had only skirted this land.

Seventeen years later another Jesuit, Antonio de Andrade, seemingly unconvinced by the dying Brother's protest that Cathay was the same country as China, set out from Agra in March 1624 in search of Christian communities beyond the Himalayas, communities that Goes had shown were a fiction of travelling merchants. His journey took him beyond Hardwar in north India, through the dominions of the rajah of Srinagar, a region never previously seen by a European, then along the difficult and rocky road following the Ganges until he reached the holy temples of Badrinath. This was a road taken by no other Europeans except the Jesuits until another European, Captain R.V. Raper, traversed it a hundred and eighty years later. But Andrade continued beyond Badrinath to Mana. From the summit of the Mana Pass, he was the first European to look down on the plains of Tibet. He can rightly be said to have discovered Tibet for the West.

From the Mana Pass Andrade went on to Tsaparang on the upper Satlej; other Jesuits followed later and established a centre in the town.

But it was not until 1661 that any European reached Lhasa. This was the achievement of two other Jesuits, one an Austrian, Johannes Grueber, the other a Belgian, Albert d'Orville. Their purpose was different from Andrade's: they set out from Peking in search of an overland route from China to India that would be less hazardous than the sea passage through the Malacca Straits. Grueber brought back sketches of Lhasa made during his brief stay in the capital. But the most informative description of the city was left to another Jesuit, an Italian, Ippolito Desideri, who reached Lhasa in March 1716 and lived there or near there for five years studying the religion, language and customs of the people. But his name and his book were unknown to the nineteenth-century English authorities in India and to the pandits collaborating with them, who tried unsuccessfully to sneak into the city but were without exception turned back. It was only in 1904 that Desideri's writings became known and were published by the Royal Geographical Society of Italy. Their publication established him beyond doubt as one of the greatest travellers in Tibet, if not the very greatest.

When Antonio de Andrade and his companions first crossed into Tibet, the land was still shrouded in mystery. They penetrated bleak mountain regions later to be known as the Roof of the World; they met men and beheld a country unseen by any European before them, and experienced hardships and dangers that would have tested mountaineers with modern equipment. Although these Jesuits at times found themselves caught up in political or local upheavals, they met only a welcoming and friendly people. At no time did they encounter the jealousy with which the Tibetans of the nineteenth century guarded their mountain passes, and especially their capital, against the intrusion of foreigners. Although Andrade published in Lisbon the first book ever written on Tibet, the reports of the Jesuits were in the first place intended for their Superiors in India or Rome: they were factual without a trace of exaggeration. In none of their writings is any tale found of encounters with wild animals such as bears, leopards and wild dogs, which can be found in recent books on the country. Not even the ubiquitous leeches are mentioned. However, like later travellers, they had their encounters with bandits.

In the strictest sense these men were pioneers: they had no precursors, no experience of others to guide them, and no maps. If the information they brought back did not satisfy cartographers, it must be remembered that they did not look on themselves as explorers. They were not equipped for scientific exploration, unlike the pandits trained by Captain T.G. Montgomerie, who were taught how to use the compass and sextant, usually hidden in a Tibetan prayer wheel, and how to calculate distances by counting their paces with a rosary. On Grueber's expedition none of the priests carried any scientific instrument or possessed any scientific training. Their aim was different.

At the time that Goes set out from Agra, the missionary vision of the Jesuits embraced four great empire: India, Ethiopia, Japan and China. Already in 1585 three Japanese princes and a party of young noblemen had visited the ageing Pope Gregory XIII under the aegis of the Jesuits in India and the Far East. In China thanks to Matteo Ricci, who had been appointed court mathematician and astronomer, the Jesuits were firmly established in the Emperor's favour. In India a priest at Akbar's court reported enthusiastically about the great Mogul: 'The Prince is friendlily disposed towards Christians and towards Señora Maria, as he calls her, and he has some fine pictures of her in his quarters. He also commends himself daily to her care.' If hopes for Akbar's conversion were idle, the Jesuits could console themselves with their success in Ethiopia, where the Emperor, the Prester John of medieval legend, petitioned the Pope in 1616 for a nuncio who could oversee the return of his country to Rome.

Only this flickering prospect of the conversion of these ancient empires to Christianity accounts for the Jesuits' travels across the roof of the world, the subject of this book.

Bento de Goes

In the town of Villa Franca do Campo on the island of San Miguel in the Azores stands a statue of a Jesuit Brother dressed as a Persian merchant with a turban, ankle-length frock, flowing beard and long hair. This is Goes, who in the first years of the seventeenth century travelled overland from India to China, skirting the borders of Tibet to the west and north. The diary in which he entered day by day the events of his journey survives only in a few fragments rescued from destruction by Isaac, his faithful Armenian companion, who later handed them over to Fr Matteo Ricci, the Jesuit astronomer in Peking. In 1583 Ricci had entered Kwangtung Province in China, where he studied the Chinese classics, adopted a Chinese name, strove for a perfect command of the language and attracted the curiosity of the Chinese with his clocks, maps, paintings and scientific instruments. Moving first to Nanch'ang, a centre of Chinese culture, he settled for some months at Nanking. Twice refused admission to Peking, he finally entered the city in May 1600 with a train of eight pack horses. Although he was not at first received by the emperor Wan-li, he was given permission to stay in the capital and within a short time had established himself as court mathematician and astronomer. It was he who with fragments of Goes's diary, with the oral account of the journey given him by Isaac, and with his own knowledge of China, pieced together as well as he could the story of Goes's truly epic journey.

A critical edition of Ricci's narrative was published by the Jesuit Fr Pietro Tacchi Venturi in 1910 to commemorate the third centenary of Ricci's death. Some missing parts of Goes's journal can be filled in from four letters that he wrote to his Jesuit friends and superiors in India during the course of his journey.

Two objectives guided Goes's journey. The first was to discover whether the Cathay of the medieval travellers was the same country as Matteo Ricci's China; the second was to search for an overland route from India to the Jesuit missions in China and Japan should Dutch Calvinist and English privateers seal off the sea passage through the Straits of Malacca.

The word Cathay or Khita was first used in the West about the tenth century for a country to the northeast of China across the Chingan Mountains. The inhabitants, known as Khitans, later extended their territory to the south into northern China as far as the left bank of the Huang-He or Yellow River. Around 1206 these people were subjugated by Genghis Khan, the Mongol conqueror, who, after taking Peking in 1215, regarded himself as ruler of Khita or Cathay.

Almost fifty years later the Flemish friar William of Rubruck described for the first time the people of this country: they were small of stature, spoke through the nose and had very narrow eyes; they wrote with pencils of the kind used by painters, and each of the characters consisted of several letters forming a whole word. Other travellers like Marco Polo returned with stories of the great number of Christians in the region: they were said to be mostly Nestorians or followers of the fifth-century heretic Nestorius, who had maintained that there were two Persons in Christ.

Towards the end of the century, Franciscans were invited to Cathay by its fabled ruler, Kublai Khan, and made sufficient progress that the Pope considered it advisable to appoint several bishops for the country under an archbishop, John de Monte Corvino, who established his see at the capital, then known as Cambaluc (Khanbalig), the city of Khan or Peking.

This missionary enterprise ended because of attacks from the southern Chinese, who expelled all foreigners, closed their frontiers and sealed themselves off from the West. When Islam, advancing through central Asia, established a series of Muslim nations about the same time, the isolation was complete: knowledge of the country became vague and fancy soon took over from fact. Cathay, nevertheless, still retained a place in the dreams of mariners who sought to find a way to the elusive land. Interest in Cathay declined further after the discovery of America. It was only late in the sixteenth century, after Jesuit missionaries had gained entry into China, that travellers began to wonder whether China might be the Cathay of the Middle Ages. Writing in October 1596 after long conversations with Persian merchants, Matteo Ricci had little doubt that the two countries were identical. Nevertheless Ricci's conclusions were not accepted. The legend of Cathay persisted and cartographers continued to place the elusive country, along with all places associated with it, to the northeast of China. Meanwhile the Portuguese were too preoccupied with their Indian possessions to concern themselves with the question.

It was a chance event at the court of Akbar, the Great Mogul, at Lahore that brought the existence of Cathay to the fore again.

With intervals there had been Jesuits at his courts both in Agra and Lahore since February 1580. Reputed a despot and known as the Terror of India, Akbar, a descendant of Genghis Khan, had conquered all northern Hindustan and had advanced as far south as the central plains of the Deccan. At the same time, Akbar was an intellectual; he was also a freethinker, anxious to examine every system of belief found among his people, hoping to reach a formula that would bring them together. He had already established a uniform system of administration in his dominions, and by enforcing a single religion was now hoping to broaden the basis of his authority.

In 1594 Akbar for the third time invited the Jesuits to Lahore to hold discussions on religion and 'instruct him in the divine law'. Two priests were appointed for the task, Jerónimo Xavier, a nephew of St Francis, and Emmanuel Pinheiro, a fluent Persian speaker. Brother Bento de Goes went with them.

Nothing is known of Goes's family or youth. Born in 1561, he was certainly given a good education. For some unknown reason he interrupted his studies in the Azores and joined the Portuguese colonial army in India. While there he sailed with the fleet to Travancore, where in the chapel at Coleche he underwent a conversion from his loose-living camp life; later, in February 1584, he entered the Jesuit novitiate at Goa. He left soon afterwards and spent some years in Ormuz before seeking readmission to the Jesuits in April 1588. He was then twenty-six. Rejecting the suggestion that he should study for the priesthood, he chose to become a Brother. He was clearly an outstanding man to have been selected for the mission to Lahore.

After a journey full of hazards across the Indian desert, the party reached Akbar's capital on 5 May 1595. Soon after their arrival, Goes was entrusted with the direction of a small school for the education of the princes of the court. Two years later he and Xavier accompanied Akbar on a tour of Kashmir. 'Being one day with the Crown Prince,' wrote Xavier, 'I saw a merchant enter the palace, a

11

man about sixty years old and a Mohammedan.' He said he came from the Kingdom of Katay and was on his return from a pilgrimage to Mecca. He had lived in the capital, Xembala, for thirteen years. It was a mighty empire with fifteen hundred cities, many of them with an immense population. A large number of the inhabitants were Isauitae, or followers of Jesus, with their own priests, sacraments and churches; there were also disciples of Moses and Mohammed. In addition, the merchant gave details of their dress and customs.

Since his information corresponded closely with much that the medieval travellers and missionaries had written about Cathay, his account was the more readily accepted; but knowing no better, he had taken Chinese Buddhism with its temples, images, and ceremonies as a form of Christianity and, like Muslim travellers before him, had come back with stories of a flourishing Christian community.

It would seem that about this time Akbar was contemplating the conquest of the whole of the Deccan, which would eventually have involved an attack on the Portuguese settlements. Goes, who must have been a man of considerable diplomatic skill, was able to dissuade him from the project and was commissioned by the Mogul to negotiate a peace treaty with the Portuguese Viceroy of India.

Meanwhile Xavier had passed on to the Provincial at Goa the information given him by the Muslim merchant. The Jesuits there had already heard similar reports of a vast country with an almost entirely Christian population beyond the mountains in the north: it had become known in Europe in the thirteenth century through the travels of Marco Polo but had been forgotten for centuries. On his return to Goa on Akbar's business, Goes first met Nicholas Pimenta, who during Goes's absence had been appointed as Visitor to report to Rome on the state of the Jesuit mission in India. Pimenta, like Goes, spoke fluent Persian, the commercial language of central Asia, and was familiar with the customs of Islam. Ricci's arguments had not convinced him that Cathay and China were identical. 'All the authors,' Ricci had written emphatically as recently as 7 September 1598,

> have stated that this great kingdom [Cathay] lies in
> this part of the world to the east of Persia and to the

south of Tartary. Now no one in China has any knowl-
edge of such a kingdom, which they would be bound
to have heard of through commerce or wars. At very
least they would have heard of its existence.
Ricci went on to say that the only indication he had found of a
Christian presence in China was a small bell with a cross and a
Greek inscription that he had seen in an antiquarian's shop in
Nanking.

On the other hand, almost every authority in the course of the
centuries had opposed such identification: the manners of the court
of Cathay differed from Ricci's reports from Peking, and all agreed
that there were at least vestiges of Christianity in Cathay. Even if
Ricci was right, the discovery of an overland route to China would
be preferable to the hazardous sea voyage.

Pimenta put the proposal to Philip II, who charged the Viceroy
to further the expedition in any way he could. The Dutch were now
searching for a route to Cathay through Muscovy and Tartary, and
the English believed that it was only a matter of time before they
would discover in the northwest a sea passage to the China seas.
For his own reasons, Akbar added his support, contributing four
hundred gold pieces to the cost and providing letters of commen-
dation to all princes on the proposed route who were either his
allies or tributaries.

Xavier meanwhile had sought further information about routes
to Cathay. In 1598 he wrote to Goa explaining that

> a traveller from Lahor must first arrive in Cachimir
> [Kashmir], which still belongs to Akbar's empire and
> from there one travels to the Kingdom of Tebat
> (Ladakh), where the ruler is a great friend of Akbar.
> And with letters provided by that prince, one arrives
> without difficulty at Caygar [Kashgar], which is only
> a few leagues from the first town in Chatai [Cathay],
> which is inhabited by Christians.

The Jesuits at Goa, however, preferred to follow the *Theatrum
Orbis Terrarum*, the first modern atlas of the world, compiled by
Abraham Ortelius, Philip II's Flemish geographer, and published in
1587. Tibet or Xavier's Tebat, a country unknown in Europe, was
not even marked on Ortelius's map of central Asia. Consequently
Xavier's proposed route was set aside and it was decided that Goes

should go via Lahore, Kabul, and Badakshan. In accordance with Ortelius's map they reckoned that the distance between Lahore and Cathay could be covered in six months.

After returning to Agra, in order to circumvent the difficulties a traveller from Europe, and particularly a Portuguese, might meet among a Muslim population, Goes adopted the disguise of a Persian merchant: he carried a scimitar, bow and quiver and allowed his hair to grow long. He did not, however, conceal that he was a Christian. Assuming the name of Abdullah Isai, he took with him a large supply of merchandise, mainly lapis lazuli, loaded on camels that he bought for the journey. For the instruction of the people of Cathay, he had with him also a letter to Matteo Ricci and a memorandum from the archbishop of Goa on the eastern schisms, together with a table of moveable feasts until the year 1620, a prerequisite for bringing separated churches into line with Rome. Two companions were assigned to him, both Greeks: Leo Grimanus, a priest who spoke Turkish, and a merchant, Demetrius. Four servants completed the company.

The party left Agra on 29 October 1602, and on 8 December arrived at Lahore, where Goes promptly dispensed with the services of the two Greeks, whom he had found useless, and engaged in their place Isaac, an Armenian Christian who lived in Lahore with his wife and children and who was to prove an invaluable companion. Devoted though Goes was to the Society, he had to shun the company of the two Jesuits living in the city for fear of revealing his identity. Instead he lodged with a Venetian merchant, Giovanni Battista Galisio.

For Goes it was a time of great loneliness. He missed especially the company of Jerónimo Xavier, with whom he had spent so many months at Akbar's court. He prayed to be granted to see him again in this life. 'Then I shall be able to sing the Canticle of Simeon,' he wrote to him, '"Now lettest thy servant depart in peace, O Lord."' He also began to wonder whether he would survive the rigours of the journey and feared for his life in the company of zealous Muslims who at any time might try to force him to apostatize.

Since the caravan for Kashgar, his immediate destination, left only once a year, it was not until 24 February that he was able to continue his journey. The caravan was made up of some five hundred merchants with servants, camels, horses and baggage.

Bento de Goes

Their route ran northwest from Lehore into the pass connecting India with Afghanistan. Drums were beaten when it was time to make camp; and again at the start of the day, they gave the signal to load the camels and carts for the road. From Kabul, Goes would make his way eastward through unmapped country.

In the first days of the journey Goes observed Lent, eating one meal, when the caravan came to a halt in the evening. 'Though we have to pay a lot for it,' he wrote in a letter several days after leaving Lahore, 'our fare consists only of a little rice with ghee, some coarse cakes *(apas)*, and some onions; if we can get a little salt fish, we count it a treat though it causes thirst. The cold is very severe, for we are passing through snow-covered mountains.' The movement of his camel made it difficult for him to read his prayers. 'Owing to the difficulties and turmoil of the journey,' he continued, 'I am unable to observe the regular times and forms of prayer. Instead, I communicate with God in my heart and thus gain strength to bear his cross.' As he prayed he would look on himself as a missionary on his way to an uncharted country that no European had yet penetrated.

After a month they reached Alhec (the modern Attock), where they crossed the Indus, at that point no more than a bow-shot in width. After defeating his rebellious brother, the Emir of Kabul, in battle, Akbar had built and fortified a town here to defend his northwest frontier, planting trees along the approach to the town to commemorate his victory. From Attock it was some fifty miles to Peshawar, their next halt. It was a perilous and difficult march in cold weather through hills infested with brigands.

Peshawar (the name Akbar gave the ancient town Purushapuru (Frontier Town), guarding as it did the narrow entrance to the Khyber Pass, had for centuries been the target of Afghan, Persian, and Mongol invaders. Akbar had strongly fortified the town on his return from Afghanistan. The Jesuit Antonio de Montserrate, who had accompanied Akbar over the pass in 1581, describes the diffi-culties the Emperor's army encountered. 'Care had to be taken,' he writes,

> to pave the road, though in a hasty manner. Even this had taxed to the utmost the skilled gangs of sappers and workmen. In spite of this, the elephants (there were a great number of them), the laden camels and

the flocks and herds found the pass most difficult and dangerous. If they had slipped, they and their riders would have been in imminent danger of death. . . . Advancing further, the army came to the narrowest part of the pass, where two high crags overhang it from either side so that a hundred stout warriors could forbid passage to many thousands. . . . Still further on we reached a precipitous slope where the animals could scarcely find a foothold, and the infantry along with the baggage train were forced to make a long detour.[1]

Two days after leaving Peshawar the caravan that Goes had joined entered the Khyber Pass and no doubt experienced similar hazards before reaching Jellalabad. Monserrate had found it an enchanting place with a pleasant climate, vineyards, gardens, pear trees, peaches, pomegranates, figs and mulberries. The streams provided the means to transport goods that were carried in oil-skins with the steersman bound to the top of the load. The people were devoted to music and sang sweetly to the pipe and lyre in free high tones in the European manner, not with the low quavering notes of the Asiatics.

Beyond Jellalabad the caravan entered the Chital Valley. To protect the travellers from marauders as they made their way through the narrow defiles, the governor of the town provided an escort of four hundred soldiers. As the caravan wended its way through the mountain ravines, the escort took to the high ground to prevent brigands from hurling down rocks on the caravan from above. All the same, travellers had at times to force their way at sword point with the loss of both merchandise and men. It was during this stage of the journey that Goes learned of worse perils ahead. 'While on their way to a small town,' Ricci wrote,

they met a wandering hermit, who told them that some thirty days' march ahead there was a territory called Caferstan which no Mohammedan was allowed to enter. Those who did get through were punished with death; heathen merchants, however, could go about unmolested though they were debarred from their temples. He added that they never entered their temples unless they were clothed in black, that the

country was fertile, and that it produced grapes in
abundance. Bento tasted of the wine that the hermit
offered him and found it in no way different from
ours. Drinking wine being contrary to all usage
among Mohammedans, he surmised that the inhabitants were Christian.

The hermit, however, added later that the people professed an
ancient Iranian religion that had held out against Islam's conquest
of central Asia.

This was clearly Kafirstan, the hilly country to the northeast of
Kabul between the river Kunar and the Hindu Kush Mountains.
The Muslims who encircled them spoke of the inhabitants as
Kaffirs or unbelievers, though they were more commonly called
Siah-Posh on account of the black garments mentioned by the
hermit. This was perhaps the first time a Westerner had noted the
existence of these people, and it was only in the nineteenth century
that travelers described them once again, remarking on their fierce
independence, their strong physique, and the fear they inspired in
their neighbors. Their hatred of the Muslims was as virulent as
ever: every Siah-Posh was reported to go bareheaded until he had
killed a Muslim and was not permitted to marry until he had killed
at least two. Eventually, six months after setting out, the caravan
reached Kabul, which Ptolemy calls Keroura.

Strategically situated seven thousand feet up in a commanding
position on the Kabul River and guarded by two fortresses, Balar
Hissar and Cherpour, it was a large, ancient, and beautiful city with
numerous caravanserais. Rebuilt several times on different sites,
the city was the pivotal point in Goes's journey; for, as Monserrate
points out, it lay 'at the very heart of the mountains that stretch out
their arms, as it were, to touch the surrounding countries, India,
Bokhera, Bactria, and Tartary'. It was through here that Alexander
the Great, Ghenghis Khan, and Babur, the founder of the Mogul
dynasty, had passed on their conquest of northern India. It was the
westernmost point of Goes's journey. Here he had to wait another
eight months while a new caravan was formed. But during the
delay Goes had one piece of good fortune: he met a sister of
Mohammed Khan, the king of Kashgar, his next immediate destination. While on her return from a pilgrimage to Mecca, the lady
had been robbed by brigands, who left her no means of paying for

the rest of her journey. Goes sold some of his lapis lazuli, loaned
her some of the money that Akbar had given him, and in company
with her and Isaac set out at the end of August 1603 on the trail to
Kashgar, normally a journey of two to three months. According to
Ricci, the caravan travelled directly north through the territory of
the Kaffirs towards the mountain range of the Hindu Kush. Others
had taken this road before him but no Christian. Goes, however,
was under the protection of Akbar, and thanks to his generous loan
to the princess, he had as it were been adopted by Islam. Their first
halt was at Charikar, a iron-mining town some forty miles from
Kabul situated at the very foot of the Hindu Kush mountain range,
the Caucasus of the ancient historians. Here Goes fell seriously ill
and, to make matters worse, clashed with the authorities, who
refused to honour Akbar's letter granting him dispensation from
all duties owed on his merchandise. However, he recovered from
his fever sufficiently to continue with the caravan when it resumed
its march after a halt of three weeks.

Rather than traverse other passes through the mountains, which
reached to sixteen thousand feet in places, the caravan made for the
pass of Parwan, which was approached by seven minor clefts
known as Haft-bachah (the seven young ones). The narrative calls
this passage 'difficult', an assessment confirmed by modern travellers. Often they had to make their way across frozen tracks, shel-
tering for days at a time from mountain storms, along zigzagging
paths up steep gorges, always in peril from avalanches. In 1847
Thomas Thomson, a surgeon in the Bengal army, while travelling
along this route continuously suffered from mountain sickness as
he ascended the pass. 'During the whole day,' he wrote,

> I was never free from a dull headache, evidently
> caused by the great elevation. Rest relieved it, but the
> least exertion brought it back again. It continued all
> evening, as long as I was awake, and still remained in
> the morning, when I rose soon after daybreak to
> prepare for the journey. A few paces took us beyond
> the shingly ravine in which we had been encamped,
> and the remainder of the ascent was throughout over
> loose angular fragments, the debris of cliffs on the
> right. Under the latter we passed, winding round the
> side of the semicircular bay till we got to about the

centre when the ascent became excessively steep and toilsome. The exertion of raising the body was very fatiguing and the last few hundred yards were only accomplished after many pauses.[2]

At Parwan, the last town under the jurisdiction of Akbar, the caravan remained five days. A short distance beyond the town began a country allied to Akbar, the kingdom of Badakshan, where Goes knew several members of the royal family: in 1595 on his first arrival at Lahore he had given lessons to three sons of its ruler, Mirza Shahruch, then an exile in India.

Here in the eastern region of Badakshanat Talashan, a town of some importance, the caravan, attacked by bandits and abandoned by the local chieftain to care for itself, drew its baggage train into a defensive circle. Overwhelmed by their attackers, all in the caravan were driven into the deserted town while their merchandise was plundered. Only a threat of retaliation from the ruler saved them from a worse fate.

In passing through this region, Goes noted that 'the inhabitants of this country, like the Flemings, were of fair complexion.' Nineteenth-century travellers later identified them as part of the freedom-loving Calcia people, who are scattered in villages of the northern Hindu Kush: they too remarked on their fair complexion, blue eyes, brown beards, and reddish hair. The meaning of their name, they explained, was 'a hungry raven forced to retire to the mountains for a livelihood'.[3]

Shortly after setting out again, the caravan was attacked a second time at a village further north and escaped only by paying the rebels a tribute on their merchandise. Some time after this incident, Goes, who was riding at a distance behind the main body, was held up by four rebels. To distract their attention momentarily, Goes took off his Persian cap in which there was a glittering stone and flung it as far away as he could. As the attackers rushed after it, Goes put spurs to his horse and made a quick getaway.

For ten days the caravan followed a precipitous path above the upper reaches of the River Oxus, finally halting at Tenghi. In places the track was so narrow that the caravan had to go in single file. Goes notes that the word *tenghi* means 'difficult': in 1271 the Venetian traveller Marco Polo had used the same word to describe the pass he had taken through these mountains.

Making slower progress than at any other time, the caravan approached the formidable Pamirs, the mountainous region located for the most part in the former Soviet Union and extending into the southwest Chinese province of Sinkiang. It is from here that the Hindu Kush, the Himalaya, and other mountain systems radiate. On the high plateau between peaks rising to more than twenty thousand feet and known as the 'Roof of the World', there were some stunted trees and grassland that supported nomadic sheep: 'neither a plain nor a down,' writes a late nineteenth-century traveller,

> nor a steppe nor a plateau, but a mountain valley of glacial formation, differing only from the adjacent or other mountain valleys in its superior altitude and in the great degree to which its trough has been filled up by glacial detritus and alluvium; it has thus approximated in appearance to a plain owing to the inability of the central stream to scour for itself a deeper channel.[4]

More recent explorers describe it as a rather irregular series of high ridges and high, level valleys, which extend over immense distances between high mountain ranges. Marco Polo had been the only European to cross this region before Goes, and it was not until the eighteen thirties that the crossing was made by another European, John Wood.

In a letter written a short time later, Goes describes this leg of his laborious journey: in the course of it Goes lost five horses through the intense cold, the lack of fodder, or the great altitude, which made it difficult for animals to breathe; both men and beasts gasped for breath, the men sustaining themselves with garlic, onions and dried apples, while they rubbed the gums of their beasts with garlic. It was a journey that took forty days in winter, though fewer in summer; and, as Goes writes, it lay through country notorious for the marauding bands that lie in wait for the caravans to rob or murder them. In fact, while these remote valleys provided pasture for the herds that sustained the sparse inhabitants known as Kirghiz, the region from time immemorial had been a refuge for criminals escaping justice. All who have ventured onto the so-called plateau, including the French explorer Bonvalot, have spoken also of the danger of mountain sickness with its accompanying compression of the lungs, bleedings, and quickened pulse.

'At last, after twenty days' march,' Ricci wrote, 'they arrived at the province of Sirikol, where they found several villages built close to one another.' Two days were allowed to rest their jaded horses and after another two days they found themselves at the foot of the Chichiklik Mountains. The pass ahead, a high, almost level plateau enclosed by mountains and swept by ice storms, lay under deep snow; during the six days' march several members of the caravan died of cold, Goes himself only barely escaping death. Yaks were unladen and driven through the snow to make a track for the travellers battling against glacial winds.

Before they reached the next halt, Tangitar, Isaac lost his foothold and was swept into the fast-flowing river between precipitous rocks. He was saved by Goes, who rushed ahead and at the next gorge rescued his friend from the torrent. Binding his wounds and lighting a fire, he sat by Isaac for eight hours until he recovered consciousness and was able to rejoin the caravan, which had continued on its way without them.

From Tangitar they went on to Yarkand, the capital of the kingdom of Kashgar and the terminus of the caravan from Kabul. Ricci cautiously estimated that Goes reached the city in November 1603, thirteen months after leaving Agra. Forming an oasis at the western end of the Takla Maklan Desert, it had for centuries been a stopping place and emporium on the famed Silk Road between China and the West. Marco Polo had visited it in 1271 and 1275, when it was subject to the Great Khan's nephew, and had found it 'amply stocked with the means of life, especially cotton, hemp, and corn, but little else worth mentioning'. But he met a number of Nestorian Christians living there. Goes, however, found only a large population of Turkic-speaking Muslims, fair-haired and music-loving, who made an easy living by farming and hunting in the nearby hills. Goes mentions also the large number of Muslim temples in the city and noted the curious ceremony they observed on Fridays: as soon as all the believers had left the great mosque after their prayers, twelve men carrying leather scourges went through the streets chastising all who had not been present, a ritual that was intended to obtain for absentees pardon for their neglect.

Here in Yarkand a Christian now went in danger of his life.

This was no new experience for Goes. Even before leaving India, while he was still in Kashmir, a rajah had threatened to have him crushed beneath the foot of an elephant in punishment for his unbelief, but his cool reply that he would gladly lay down his life for the true God averted the menace. On another occasion some hostile Muslims, sword in hand, had tried to get him to call upon Mohammed, but again they had respected his courage and desisted. While Goes did not openly flaunt his religion, he did not conceal it. The inhabitants of Yarkand called him an Armenian Roumi, for they still after thirteen centuries identified people of Armenia with the Byzantine neighbors of the Parthian Empire.

Summoned to appear before the ruler, Sultan Mohammed, a descendant of Genghis Khan, he was asked whether he was a follower of Moses or David or Mohammed and in what direction he faced when he prayed. He answered that his faith was in Jesus and that he did not mind where he faced in prayer because God was everywhere. This set the mullahs debating the statement; but while they could not deny it, they nevertheless tried to convert him, telling him that they could not understand why a man who was so obviously intelligent could profess any religion other than their own. But outside in the streets he had several times to escape the scimitars of fanatical believers who tried to make him invoke the Prophet.

During his prolonged stay in the city, Goes came to know a merchant from Moscow whom he had seen making the sign of the cross. One morning the Russian came to him in great distress. Leading Goes back to his lodging, he showed him his small son lying there very seriously sick. Through gestures Goes indicated that he thought that the child might need some new medicine. But the Russian made it clear that everything had been tried and that the boy was no better. He wanted Goes only to pray. Bento placed his breviary on the boy's head, hung a cross round his neck and knelt by his bed in prayer. Three days later the Russian, bringing the boy with him, came to Goes in the house he had rented in the city, carrying with him presents to thank him for his prayers.

To his delight, Goes found that the people of Yarkand had heard of the country called Cathay, which, they told him, lay several months' journey to the east. It was only rarely that a caravan travelled there, and the next one to go in that direction would not depart for another twelve months.

The organization of a caravan for Cathay followed strict regulations. The right of marshalling and leading it was granted by the sultan to the highest bidder, who paid him two hundred bags of musk. With absolute authority over it, the leader then associated with himself four others who were given the title of ambassadors, and then enrolled seventy-two travellers who had to buy their admission. The caravan then had the appearance of an embassy, for this was the only way it could enter China.

Ricci explains this face-saving system. 'Most merchants,' he writes,

> coming into this town [Su-cheu, the modern Jiu Quan] arrive from the west as though they were ambassadors. There are seven or eight countries that have obtained the right from the Chinese government for seventy-two persons under the guise of ambassadors to bring their tribute to the King every five years. This tribute is paid in transparent marble (jade or nephrite), diamonds, blue pigments and similar articles. As the King considers it incompatible with his dignity to accept anything from foreigners without payment, he lodges and entertains them lavishly at his expense and gives them a gold piece each day; and this is why it is only possible to join the caravan by giving its leader gifts or cash. On the day they leave, they present their forged letters patent to the Chinese sovereign, paying him their respectful homage. Embassies of this kind are admitted from several countries, such as Cochin-China, Siam, Korea, the Riukiu Islands, and from some small Tartar princes. All this is an immense burden on the treasury, but the Chinese who are well aware of the deception, want to flatter their sovereign in this way, making him believe that the whole world pays tribute to China, while in fact it is China that pays tribute to these countries.

Many examples of this 'tribute' paid by the ambassadors are extant; thus, for example, the Hafiz Khan, the 'ambassador' from Samarkand, presented six Arab horses and a hundred small knives, and asked in return for brocade, satin and tea; others would request blue porcelain bowls, muslin, linen and other cloth, usually after presenting horses, jade and knives in exchange.

In Yarkand Goes came to know a Tibetan chieftain who three years earlier had been taken prisoner. Goes visited him in jail and questioned him about his country, making use of an interpreter, the King's physician, who spoke Persian. The Tibetan told him that their chief Father wore a mitre on his head and was robed in a chasuble; the people fasted for forty days, taking neither wine nor meat; their priests were celibate and followed a sacred book called the *Kanjur*, which Goes thought might be the Bible, and believed in a day of judgement and in several hells and heavens. Excited by what he heard, Goes noted down all the details he could discover about these people, thinking that they might be some ancient forgotten Christians.

Having gathered from merchants in Yarkand all the information he could about Cathay, Goes thought he might have found evidence of the existence of Christians in that country in their porcelain as well as in their paintings and decorated fans. He was shown one painting in particular of a man wearing a biretta on which there appeared to be a representation of the crucified Christ, with another figure kneeling in the foreground with hands crossed on his chest; and he also discovered a piece of porcelain on which there was a figure that looked like a Franciscan friar with a long beard and tonsured head.

In the course of his long wait in Yarkand, Goes went to Khotan at the invitation of the princess, the sister of the King of Kashgar, whom he had befriended at Kabul after she had been robbed on her way back from a pilgrimage to Mecca; the lady was also a close friend of the King of Khotan. The visit entailed a trip of ten days across a wind-swept desert where the dunes, rising at times to three or more metres, advanced like waves under the north wind; in other places the going was over hard, flat ground covered with gravel or white hillocks. Cut off by the desert from the busy caravan route, the city was commercially undeveloped. Here Buddhism with a blend of Nestorianism had held up the advance of Islam, so that, in contrast with natives of Yarkand, the Muslims living here were devout, like the Queen, and not aggressive.

Throughout Asia, Khotan was famous for its jade, the Yu-stone of the Chinese, the jaspis of the ancients, called nephrite by the mineralogists. It was highly valued, especially by the Chinese, who used it to make vases, bracelets and ornaments for clothes, enhancing them with engravings of leaves and flowers. After Marco Polo, Bento de Goes was the first European to visit Khotan, and it is here that his reconstructed narrative is fuller than in other places.

The most valuable stone was obtained from the River Khotan, which ran close to the capital. Goes stood and watched it being gathered somewhat in the manner of divers fishing for pearls. It was generally brought up in the form of large pebbles, vermilion, green, grey and black. The less valuable kind was extracted from the mountains some twenty days' journey from the capital, then cut into large slabs about six feet wide for transportation.

The Queen repaid Goes in the very finest jade, white with rose-coloured specks and green veined with gold.

After its leader, Agi Afis, had invited Goes to join the ambassadorial party, he purchased eleven horses for himself, Isaac and his merchandise; he had bartered what remained of his lapis lazuli for jade, which was more sought-after in Cathay.

Some time in the autumn of 1604, the caravan began its march for Cathay with several hundred animals loaded with merchandise and skins filled with water. Their way led across the Takla Maklan Desert, bounded on all sides except the northeast by mountain ranges. Ricci was perhaps the first Westerner to call attention to the charm of the names given to all the sand-swept small towns in oases between Yarkand and Ak-su (A-Ko-Su): Tallik, the place of willows, Ming-jigda, the thousand white poplars, Chilan, the jujube tree and others that are difficult to identify, for Ricci was relying on the memory of Isaac the Armenian.

Aksu, set on a river of the same name at the centre of an oasis lying at the foot of the Tien-Shan Mountains, was another caravan hub on the old Silk Road: its king was a boy of twelve and a cousin of the King of Kashgar. He gratefully accepted sugar, sweets, and other presents suitable to his years and had a festive dance performed in the presence of Goes; then he invited his guest to do a Portuguese dance, something he had not done since his days in the army. To show his appreciation, the King exempted Goes from the levy on his goods. After a visit to the King's mother and a delay of fifteen days to allow stragglers to catch up with the caravan, they moved on to Kucha, where they took a whole month's rest. As Ricci's narrative indicates, the travellers had great need of this respite, because 'the difficult journey, the heavy load of marble, and the want of food had exhausted everyone's strength.' Probably no member of the caravan was more glad to move on than Goes, who had been fined and chastised during his stay there for refusing to observe Ramadan.

Passing through a fortified town, probably Korla, they continued to Karashan, a pleasant town set beside a lake. Isaac later narrated to Ricci the hardship endured on this last march through the desert, the burning sun, sand storms, lame ponies, the hard night frosts. Here the leader decided on a long wait, hoping to collect the full complement allowed by China for the caravan in order to increase his profits. After three months Goes's patience could hold out no longer. With the King's permission he decided to continue alone. But as he was about to set out, a large party arrived from Cathay with the very information Goes so much wanted.

These merchants coming from the east had entered the capital of Cathay as ambassadors and had lived there for three months with Ricci and his companions. They were unable to give Goes their European names (they had assumed new names in the Chinese fashion), but they were able to describe their appearance sufficiently to leave him in no doubt who they were; they had often been admitted to the Emperor's presence. The merchants, moreover, gave details of the presents they had given the Emperor, clocks, a clavichord, paintings and other treasures; they were even able to show Goes a scrap of paper they had picked up from the floor of Ricci's room with some Portuguese written on it, in order to prove when they got home that people using that language had penetrated China. Goes was now convinced that Cathay differed from China only in name, that Cambaluc, the capital, was Peking, and, above all, that the vast numbers of forgotten Christians with all their temples was a myth.

In spite of Agi Afis's opposition, Goes managed to obtain a passport from the local authorities; with Isaac and a small party of merchants, he continued his journey and reached the fortified town of Turfan (Tu-lu-fan). From there he went on to Chami (Hami), where he arrived on 17 October 1605. This fertile oasis was famed for its hospitality and white-fleshed melons. Marco Polo, who had stayed here for a month, found the people very gay folk who gave no thought to anything but making music, singing, and dancing. 'I give my word,' he wrote,

> that if any stranger comes to a house here to seek hospitality, he receives a very warm welcome. Then he leaves the house and goes about his own business and stays away two or three days. Meanwhile, the guest . . . does what he will with his wife, lying with her in one bed just as if she were his own wife. All the men in this city are thus cuckolded by their wives; but they are not the least ashamed of it. And the women are beautiful, vivacious, and ready to oblige.

Like Marco Polo, Goes remained a month in the town resting his horses before setting out for the western and sandy wastes of the great Gobi Desert, where the grassy fringe supported small Mongolian tribes and where intermittent streams fell into small salt lakes or disappeared into the sand. As Goes wrote, this stretch of the country was notorious for its Tartar brigands,

> so that traders always crossed it in the greatest fear, sometimes even under cover of night and in the strictest silence. Often one comes across the dead bodies of Mohammedans who have attempted the journey unaccompanied, though on the other hand the Tartars do not usually kill the native population, for they regard them as their servants and herdsmen and steal their flocks from time to time.

During the day they posted a lookout on the summit of the sand hills close to where they were camping, unable to light fires for lack of fuel; at night they marched into the cold prevalent northwest wind. For three hundred miles by the shortest route, they trekked across the sandy waste following the route of the all-conquering Ghenghis Khan; finally, as they approached the River Sulei, they met some living things, scrub, reeds, and stunted trees. At last they reached Kiayukwan (Jia-yua-guan) and came in sight of the Great Wall. There they were held up for twenty-five days while waiting for permission to go on to Su-cheu (Soo-chou).

Su-cheu with its neighboring city, Kanchow, was a garrison town supplying troops whose task it was to keep watch on the length of the Great Wall. The old town, with ornate gardens and numerous canals, was famous for its silks and embroidery, and had for centuries been an important trading centre. Foreigners, mainly traders and bankers, lived in their own section of the city, carefully guarded by the Chinese and locked up at night. It was here in the predominantly Muslim enclave, that Goes lodged on entering the city about Christmas 1605.

Here again he met some merchants coming from Peking. His first task was to inform Ricci, who had been told about his mission, that he had arrived in China; this would come as no surprise to Ricci, who in a letter written to the Jesuits at Goa as recently as 12 November of that year, had reaffirmed his conviction of the identity of China and Cathay.

Goes had gained nothing by travelling ahead of the main caravan: he could get no further until its leader, Agi Afis, arrived with the papers signed by the King of Kashgar authorizing the ambassadors to offer tribute to the Emperor. These papers had to be forwarded to Peking, a thousand miles away, and returned with permission to proceed. This would take three years.

Immediately on arrival at Su-cheu, Goes wrote to Ricci in Peking. For months Ricci had been waiting for word from Goes. Whenever a foreign caravan arrived in Peking, he sought news of him, for he had been told in letters from Goa that Goes had set out from Agra in search of Cathay.

But Goes's letter from Su-cheu did not reach him, for the Brother did not know Ricci's Chinese name and had not written the address in Chinese characters. It was eleven months later, in November 1606, that a Muslim merchant handed Ricci a second letter, written on Easter day of that year. 'I am a member of the Society of Jesus,' Goes wrote,

> I was sent by my superiors to discover Cathay, but I
> now believe that no such country exists; for I have
> traversed Asia without finding it, and this country
> which in Europe we call China is known to the people
> of central Asia as Cathay. I have found no Christians
> in spite of the tales told by so many Mohammedans. I
> beg you, Fathers, or any other Portuguese or Christ-
> ians in Peking, to help me escape from the hands of
> the infidels. I have suffered greatly on the journey. I
> am exhausted and wish to return to India by the sea

route. If I wait until the caravan is allowed to proceed
to the capital, I shall be here two years, for that is the
customary delay.

Although winter conditions would add to the hardships of the
journey, Ricci immediately dispatched to Su-cheu his most trusted
pupil, John Fernandes, a young man of twenty-five who could
speak Portuguese; he sent along with him a Chinese candidate for
the Society. In company with a northern-Chinese servant, Fernandes left Peking on 11 December 1606. He would reach Goes at the
end of March 1607, only to find him close to death.

Meanwhile at Su-cheu Goes had endured worse hardships than
any he had suffered on his long journey. He had arrived in good
health with his faithful Isaac, his five servants from Yarkand, thirteen horses, and some of the finest jade. But the Muslims in Agi
Afis's caravan began persecuting him relentlessly. They constantly
forced him to lend them money that they had no intention of repay-
ing and arranged lavish banquets for themselves at his expense; the
captain himself threatened to leave him behind unless he lent him
more and more money. In the end Goes was forced to bury under
the flagstones of his house what inferior jade he had left, so that he
could pay for his journey to Peking.

Left hungry and almost penniless, Goes grew daily weaker. In
his last letter to Ricci he had written, 'You should never trust the
Mohammedans; my journey has been very long, difficult, and
dangerous, and I advise no one to undertake it again.' Nor had
Fernandes's journey been easy: his Chinese servant had stolen half
his money and left him to continue alone. The night before
Fernandes arrived, Goes saw in a dream that an answer had come
from Peking, and he told his faithful Isaac to go into the market
place and seek out the messenger.

When Fernandes entered his room, he found Goes too weak to
move. But as he spoke to him in Portuguese, the sick Jesuit's
strength returned. Unable to find a doctor, Fernandes nursed the
sick Brother as tenderly as he could: he tried to nourish him with
morsels of chicken and to revive his spirits, but his patient was at
the end of his strength. Hourly he became weaker. After ten days
he died in Fernandes's arms. It was 11 April 1608.

The Muslims who had been with Goes in the caravan immediately began to sack his house. They tore to pieces the diary he had

kept of the journey, with his records of distances, roads, their condition, and his observations on places and people. Unfortunately in
its last pages Goes had noted all the loans he had made since his
arrival at Su-cheu, which the Muslims were anxious to destroy so
that their debts could not be reclaimed. Fernandes and Isaac,
however, managed to retrieve a few crumpled and mutilated pages
together with some articles to which the Muslims attached no
value. It was their intention to have him buried according to their
religious rites in their part of the town, making out that he was one
of them, so that what was left of his possessions would revert to
them. However, Isaac and Fernandes stood firm. Purchasing a
coffin, they buried him in the Chinese section of the city and recited
a rosary over his grave. Goes's lingering illness together with the
behavior of the Muslims after his death aroused suspicions that he
had been poisoned, suspicions that Ricci was inclined to believe.

The Muslims now turned against Isaac, had him imprisoned,
then tried to get him to invoke Mahommet in one last attempt to
claim for themselves what remained of Goes's jade. The young
Fernandes, who had been taught a little Persian, stood by Isaac and
demanded that the governor of Su-cheu should hold an inquiry.
When the governor refused, Fernandes appealed to the viceroy of
Kancheu, three days' journey away, and was granted his request.
But the Muslims, knowing that Isaac was anxious to go on to
Peking as quickly as possible, tried to wear him down: they bribed
the governor to delay the process. But Isaac, who had already been
delayed six months, devised a plan to bring the matter to a conclu-
sion. When he was next summoned to court in company with
Fernandes, the two of them produced a large piece of pork and
started eating it. The Muslims cried traitor and fled.

After five months in prison, Isaac was released and given back
what remained of Goes's possessions. Meanwhile in Peking Ricci
had been waiting for twelve and a half months for news from Su-
cheu: the letters Fernandes had written had been lost. Then on 29
October 1607, exactly five years to the day after Goes had set out
from Agra, Isaac and Fernandes arrived in Peking. As Ricci saw
them approach, he dismantled the Chinese triumphal arch he had
prepared for Goes's arrival and received from the hands of Isaac
the gold crucifix Goes had worn throughout the journey and the
passports given him by Akbar the Great and the rulers of Kashgar

and Khotan, with the letters he had treasured from his friend, Jerónimo Xavier.

Ricci then wrote a letter to Goa pointing out that Goes's journey had proved beyond any doubt that Cathay and China were not two different countries and that the Christians of Cathay were probably the descendants of medieval converts. Then with the help of Isaac's recollections and the fragments of Goes's diary, he pieced together an account of their journey. Finally, after making sure that Isaac was amply recompensed for his fidelity, Ricci arranged for him to sail from Macao to rejoin his wife in India. In the Straits of Malacca his ship was captured by the Dutch, but the captain was so impressed by Isaac's story that he asked him to write it down and then set him free.

Goes's journey had achieved its twofold, albeit negative, objective: he had established that Cathay was identical with China and that the two names for the same country resulted from a confusion: in central Asia the country had been called Khita from the tenth century on after a tribe known as Khitans that had invaded northern China; this name, Khita, which was written as Cathay in Europe, the Arabs, Persians, and Russians used to designate the country. Marco Polo and the friars before him, approaching the country from the west, had therefore referred to it as Cathay, a name unknown to the Chinese themselves. They knew their country either as the Middle Kingdom or by the name of the ruling dynasty. On the other hand, the Portuguese, sailing to China through the Straits, called the country Chin or China, as it was known in Siam and Cochin-China.

Goes had also shown that any overland route from India to China was impracticable. From the sunlit plains of Hindustan, he had climbed to the heights of Central Asia, crossing four thousand kilometres of high mountain plateaus and sand-swept deserts. The first European in modern times to enter China from the West, he had placed a large section of central Asia on the map of the world and had marked it for the first time with towns, rivers, and mountains that previously had no place on it. Three hundred years later a British traveller, Sir Aurel Stein, reflected on Goes's achievement during a visit to Su-cheu. 'I had thought of him,' Stein writes,

and his plucky perseverance at all points—Lahore, Peshawar, the Pamirs, Sarikol, Yarkand, and Khotan—

where I had touched the line of his wanderings. . . . There is nothing to suggest even approximately where his wearied limbs were laid to rest by the young Chinese convert [Fernandes] whom the Jesuits had dispatched from Peking to relieve him and arrived just a few days before all earthly troubles were ended.

'Had [Goes's] diary, which he is said to have kept in great detail, been spared,' wrote another Englishman, Colonel Sir H. Yale, 'it would probably have been to this day far the most geographical record in any European language on the subject of the countries through which he travelled, still so imperfectly known.'[5]

The evidence of Goes's journey, confirming as it did Ricci's repeated assertion of the identity of Cathay and China, was not immediately accepted, in spite of yet another letter he wrote to Goa after Bento de Goes's death: 'As for Christians who are said to exist mainly in the two provinces of Chensi and Honan,' Ricci wrote,

the brethren who were dispatched there discovered nothing except that in the past there had been many Christian families in these provinces: they had prac-tised their religion for about fifty years, but the Chinese terrorized them, threatening to kill them as the descendants of the Tartars. . . . They all scattered, renounced their faith, and today none will acknowl-edge their origin.

This without doubt explains the fate of the Nestorians and Manicheans mentioned by Marco Polo in the time of the Mongol dynasty. When in 1368 the Mongols were replaced by the Ming dynasty which lasted until 1643, Christian communities suffered the same fate as the Mongols; a national reaction then swept away all, Christians included, associated in any way with it. Since Ricci's time further evidence of Christians living in Cathay has been unearthed in the form of medals, crosses and even tombs.

Cathay and its long forgotten Christian communities, as will be seen, remained too firmly lodged in the imagination of the West, and even in Goa among later generations of Goes's brethren.

[1]A. Monserrate, *The Commentary on His Journey to the Court of Akbar* (Oxford,1922),143.
[2]Thomas Thomson, *Western Himalaya and Tibet* (London, 1852), 135.
[3]Thomas Holditch, 'The Origins of the Kaffirs in the Hindu Kush', *Geographical Journal* 7 (1896).
[4]George N. Curzon, 'The Pamirs and the Sources of the Oxua', *Geographical Journal* 8 (1896), 31.
[5]Col. Sir H. Yale, *Cathay and the Way Thither*, 2:536.

Antonio de Andrade

Still in search of Christians living beyond the Himalayas, the Portuguese Jesuit Fr Antonio de Andrade made an epic journey into Tibet. Scaling the summit of the Mana Pass, eight hundred metres higher than Mont Blanc, he was the first European to gaze on the mountain world of Tibet from the heights of the Himalayas.

Andrade's account of his journey first appeared in Lisbon in 1626 under the title *Novo Descobrimento do gram Cathayo ou Reinos de Tibet, pello Padre Antonio de Andrade da Companhia de Jesu, no anno de 1626*. The book follows closely the report on Tibet which he wrote on 8 November 1624, at Agra for the Jesuit headquarters at Goa on his return to India. Its publication followed close on the celebration of the *annus mirabilis* in modern Portuguese history. In 1625 Elizabeth, daughter of Peter II of Aragon (she had died in 1336), was canonized by Pope Urban VIII, setting as it were a seal upon the recent union of Spain and Portugal under a single crown. In April of the same year, Bahia, the capital of Brazil, which had been founded by the Portuguese in 1549, was recaptured from the Dutch. And perhaps most important of all, the united kingdom of Spain and Portugal rejoiced over the union of the ancient church of Ethiopia with the See of Rome, the joint achievement of missionaries of the two countries. And now news came that in 1624 a Portuguese had discovered Tibet, an event now acclaimed as comparable to the discovery of the New World at the close of the fifteenth century.

The Italian edition of the book, which adheres more closely to Andrade's dispatch, was published in Rome in 1627 without any such fanfare. Eight years later there were translations of the book into French, Spanish, German and Dutch. The early editions end with an excited statement that 'in letters received from India it is known that Andrade has returned to Tibet with other priests from the Province of Goa.' Andrade had stirred the curiosity of Europe in his discovery.

There is a portrait of Andrade in the Academy of Science in Lisbon. Painted probably in Goa, it acclaims him the 'explorer and discoverer of Tibet'. The portrait was the gift of his great-nephew, Signor Rebelo d'Albuquerque, who had it from his uncle, the viscount d'Oleiros: this would seem to suggest that Andrade, who was born in Oleiros in 1590, came from the leading family of that small town in the province of Beira Baixa. The date of Andrade's death is given as 1634 at the age of fifty-three.

In the portrait Andrade is wearing the black soutane and cloak which was the common dress of the Jesuits at that time. He has a short black beard, black hair and black moustache, dark penetrating eyes, and arched eyebrows indicating strength of will. In his general appearance he is not unlike the man who very likely was his forebear, Alfonso de Albuquerque, the great navigator and founder of Portuguese power in the East.

Antonio de Andrade entered the Society of Jesus at Coimbra on 15 December 1596 Four years later he embarked at Lisbon for India, sailing in the *S. Valenino* with the new viceroy, Ayres de Saldanha, who was shortly to sponsor Bento de Goes's overland journey to China. The fleet raised anchor on 22 April 1600, and on 6 January 1601 reached Goa, where Andrade completed his studies for the priesthood.

Having worked in the Salsette Peninsula for some years, he was sent in 1621 to Agra to take charge of the mission established there at the court of the Mogul Emperor.

After exploring the Indian Ocean in the fifteenth century, the Portuguese were disappointed not to find anywhere, with the exception of Malabar and Socotra, any traces of an early Christianity. Goes's epic journey had proved that no Christian communities existed in central Asia. But there still remained the regions beyond the Himalayas which he had only skirted, where no European had penetrated in modern times. Muslim traders with only sketchy knowledge of Christian rites and practices continued to visit Agra with tales of a vast Christian country through which they had travelled.

When Andrade was given the opportunity to investigate for himself the truth of these persistent reports, he was quick to take it. On 30 March 1624, he left Agra to follow the Emperor on his journey to Kashmir. On reaching Delhi he learned that a large party of Hindus was about to start out on a pilgrimage to a famous shrine in the Himalayas, a journey of about two and a half months; for the first part of his journey, their company would provide him with the protection and guidance he needed. With a Brother companion, Manuel Marques, and two servants, Andrade joined the pilgrim party, so well disguised as a Hindu that his Christian acquaintances in Delhi did not recognize him.

Taking the shortest route to the shrine, the pilgrims would have followed the valley of the Ganges and reached Hardwar on the borders of Hindustan in fifteen days. There at the foot of the mountains began the territory of the rajah of Srinagar, a city founded some twenty years earlier on the left bank of the River Alaknanda, the main tributary of the Ganges: it was the principal shrine of northwest India, the city of Sri, the goddess of prosperity and beauty.

But already Andrade's fellow travellers had seen through his disguise; it was clear to them that he and his companion were neither pilgrims nor merchants. Consequently they were arrested as spies. But when no evidence could be brought against them, they were set free and allowed to continue with the caravan.

At Hardwar the Himalayas began to rise in front of them. So far no European had set foot in this vast range of mountains. The ascent of the first hills was more difficult than Andrade had anticipated; ridge rose behind ridge and the paths were so narrow that the pilgrims could advance only by inches, clinging to the wall of the rock, while far below them the sacred Ganges, rushing through a narrow gorge, seethed and foamed. To hearten one another the Hindus never ceased calling out the name of their sacred shrine with the never ending refrain, 'Ye, Badrinate, ye, ye.' Wherever the terrain allowed, there were temples, small architectural masterpieces, where a group of yogis, the well-known fanatical Hindu self-torturers, guarded the god that was worshipped there.

At this point in his narrative, Andrade digresses to tell a story about the emperor and a yogi. One day when the emperor was out hunting in Kashmir near a sacred lake, he saw a yogi of very uncouth appearance: the man was naked, his hair was more than four cubits in length and his nails were longer than the palm of his hand. A crowd had gathered round him and were worshipping his feet. The yogi took no notice of the emperor as he passed. On his return from the hunt, the emperor summoned the yogi, who refused to move unless he was carried or fetched in the royal coach. In the end the man was dragged by the hair to the emperor, who gave orders that his hair and nails should be cut and that he should be exhibited in that state at the side of the road.

As Andrade continued on his way, he was overcome by the grandeur of the scenery. The lower slopes of the mountains were covered with primeval forest, gigantic pine trees that he estimated were 'two or three times the height of the tower of the Jesuit church in Goa' and by cinnamon trees, cypress, lemon and chestnut, and by countless different flowers. Eventually the pilgrims reached Srinagar, the capital of Kashmir, a new town founded earlier in the century. Here the river, which flows far below the road, was so confined by high cliffs that it appeared like a canal hewn through the mountain.

During the halt at Srinagar, which later Jesuit travellers found so picturesque, Andrade came under suspicion for the second time. Without merchandise he could not claim to be a trader and had no alternative but to confess frankly the purpose of his journey. However, after five or six days' detention, during which several of his possessions were confiscated, he was released. For the next fifteen days the party continued up ever rising paths until it reached the first snow-covered hills, their summit sometimes buried in the clouds. But the pilgrim path wound upwards towards Joshimath, a settlement some twenty-three hundred metres above sea level. Andrade describes here in a few sentences the perils of this journey. 'We had to cross and recross the Ganges, not just by difficult bridges of rope, but by others formed by frozen masses of snow stretching the entire width of the river, while underneath its waters broke into a foaming passage. Travelling like this for a month and a half, we reached at length the shrine of Badrid.' This was the farthest limit of the territories of the rajah of Srinagar. It was the end of May or the beginning of June 1624.

It was to be almost a hundred and ninety years before another European, with the exception of Jesuits, visited this sacred place of pilgrimage. In 1812 Captain F.V. Raper published his report on the journey that he had made ten years earlier in search of the source of the Ganges. The author makes no mention of Andrade in his account, but his description of the flora, the mountain ranges, the rope bridges, and numerous small details confirm the accuracy of the Jesuit's journal. 'The road is winding,' Raper wrote, 'with steep ascents and descents, and in some parts not a little dangerous, being formed on a ledge of rock with here and there a small projecting point, not above five or six inches wide, to rest the foot upon;' and he added that in some places the path was not more than the palm of the hand in width and lay three or four thousand feet above the bed of the river.[1]

Before continuing his journey, Andrade visited the shrine. 'The temple itself,' he wrote,

> is situated at the foot of a rock from which several springs issue, one of which is so hot that it is impossible for the hand to endure the heat of the water even for a moment. This spring divides into three rivulets which flow into their separate basins. In these basins the hot water is tempered with cold from another spring so that it is just about as hot as the pilgrims can bear when they bathe in the water to cleanse their souls. The Brahmins explain the origin of the spring in this way: the element Fire, in distress at all the destruction it had done on earth, burning down houses, forests and fields, came to this temple in search of a cure for its affliction. If it were to obtain pardon, then it would have to stay. So stay it did at the feet of the god and heated the water of the spring. But one-fifteenth part of it refused to submit and still stalks the earth causing destruction wherever it goes.

Although for all but three months of the year the temple was covered or actually buried in snow, Andrade noticed that in the course of centuries 'immense treasures' had been offered to the god. Of all the temples in India this was the most sacred. Raper was told that it attracted between forty-five and fifty thousand pilgrims in the few months of the year during which it could be approached and that it possessed more beneficed lands, some seven hundred villages in all, than any other sacred Hindu shrine in the same part of India.

'Three times a day,' wrote another Jesuit, Francisco de Azevedo, who visited the shrine soon after Andrade,

> food is offered to the god, in the morning four measures of the best rice with some cocoa nuts, a large quantity of butter and some cake, at midday four

handfuls of boiled rice and many spices, and in the afternoon some refreshments. All this is placed before the god, whereupon the doors are closed; after a while the good things are taken away and divided among the Brahmin and his ministers, for the god is satisfied with the odour alone. . . . The mountain district of the pagoda is a sacred place where the criminals of the surrounding country may live unmolested. Like the ministers, however, they live a great distance away, for the god will not allow the proximity of any man or woman who is not perfectly chaste.

The same Jesuit was also told that the concourse of pilgrims was largest every twelfth year and that in 1630 the shrine was visited by eighty thousand pilgrims, including eight thousand yogis carrying arms. As the rajah of Srinagar did not care for such a regiment of armed vagabonds, he ordered them to deliver up their weapons. When they refused, the whole troop was dispersed by force.

When the snows buried the shrine, the inhabitants left the region and travelled for three or four days to villages on lower slopes of the mountains. Andrade noted how these people differed both in language and customs from all others he had met in India: they lived principally on rice, herbs and mutton, which gave them greater strength than the Hindus. He was astonished at the way they consumed snow. 'Once I saw a child,' he wrote, 'about two or three years old with a lump of snow in its hands. As I was afraid it would harm its health, I took away the snow and gave it some raisins; but it had hardly tasted them when it threw them away and cried for snow.' Andrade found it curious that the women cultivated the soil while the men did the weaving: it was the way of life of these people, the Bhutia, a tribe living on the frontiers of India and mentioned for the first time here by any traveller. Raper also noted their fine physique, men resembling the Tartars, strong, well formed and of middle height. At that time as today the men of the tribe travelled in summer to trade in southern Tibet and in winter crossed into India. During the hot weather many of them not engaged in trade lived in small villages above ten thousand feet; their homes, roofed with shingle or stone, were guarded by fierce, shaggy-coated dogs, which both medieval and modern travellers have mentioned.

Andrade now stood on the northern slopes of the Himalayas. Continuing a little northward, he came to the village of Mana, which lay past the extreme limit of Raper's journey. 'Immediately beyond this place,' Andrade writes,

there rise lofty mountains behind which lies an awful desert that is passable only during two months of the year. The crossing takes twenty days. There is a total absence of trees and plants and human habitations, and the snowfall is almost uninterrupted. As there is no fuel to be had, travellers take with them nothing that has to be cooked but live on roasted barley meal, which they mix with water and then drink. According to the natives, many die from the noxious fumes that rise from the ground; certainly it is true that many persons who are in good health are taken suddenly ill and die within a quarter of an hour, but I myself think this is due to the intense cold and to the lack of meat that reduces the heat of the body.

Others ascribed the sickness to the vapours from carbonic acid springs. However, Andrade may only be describing the ordinary symptoms of mountain sickness.

While waiting for several days for a caravan to form or for some other opportunity to cross into Tibet, Andrade was told that the rajah of Srinagar had given orders that he should be forbidden to proceed any further. Taking a grave risk, however, Andrade decided to continue alone. Leaving his companion, Manuel Marques, behind, he set out with two Christian servants and a guide. For two days he pushed on as fast as he could, but on the third morning he was overtaken by three natives who had been dispatched by the local ruler. They first informed the guide that his wife and children had been imprisoned and that he himself would certainly be executed if he did not return immediately. Andrade was then threatened: he was told that Manuel Marques would be held answerable if he disobeyed and his possessions would be confiscated; in any case, he was certain to die if he continued on his way at that time of the year.

The guide returned. Andrade went on with the two Christians. The going was terrible. At times they sank into the snow up to their chest or even to their shoulders. In some places they could make their way only by stretching out flat on the snow and propelling themselves with their hands and feet. One night they had just encamped when they were overtaken by such a heavy snowstorm that they could not see one another, although they were lying close together. The intense cold numbed their hands and faces to such a degree that when Andrade knocked his finger against some hard object, he lost part of it. 'As I had no sense of pain,' he writes,

I would not have believed it possible if it had not been
for the copious flow of blood. Our feet were frozen
and so swollen that we had no sensation when later
they touched a piece of red-hot iron. And in addition
to all this, we felt a great aversion to food of any kind
and had a violent thirst that was relieved hardly at all
by eating snow. There was in fact water, but it flowed
a great depth beneath the snow like the Ganges itself.
. . . In this way the journey continued to the summit of
the mountain range, where the river takes its rise from
a large pond and it is from there also that another river
springs and waters the regions of Tibet.

This, of course, was only one of the sources of the Ganges. Andrade, now at the highest point on his journey, at the summit of the Mana Pass, was looking down from more than eighteen thousand feet on the plains of Tibet. 'It was all one dazzling whiteness to our eyes, which had been weakened by snow blindness,' he writes, 'and we could see no indication of the road we had to follow.' One night Andrade's two companions became so weak that he decided to send them back to Mana to get help. It would take them ten days, and in the meantime he would keep some provisions with him and remain where he was awaiting their return. But the next morning the two servants either would not or dared not set out without him, so Andrade was left with no choice but to return to Mana with them. Their frost-bitten feet made progress extremely slow. Even now they might have died if after three days they had not met a Bhutian who had been sent in search of them by the people of Mana: they were afraid that they would be held responsible by the King of Tibet for any misadventure that might befall a stranger. After another three days' march, they came to some caves that they made their temporary shelter. Here they were joined by Manuel Marques, who brought with him some provisions. All four now waited for the snows to melt sufficiently for them to continue on their way. They were also suffering from snow blindness, although they shaded their eyes with guards made of gauze.

While they were getting ready to continue their journey, two guides arrived sent by the 'King of Tibet': Andrade had been careful to inform him of his coming. With the guides and with the three horses that the guides brought, they were at last able to continue their journey, and early in August 1624 they entered the royal city, the Tibetan town of Tsaparang, in the valley of Langtschen-Kamba or Upper Sutlej. Oderic de Pordenone, the Italian fourteenth-century friar, had been the only European to reach Tibet before Andrade, but he had set out from China and had not entered the Sutlej basin. It was to be another two hundred years before another European, again with the exception of Jesuits, penetrated so far into this part of the country.

'The kingdom [Tsaparang],' wrote Fr Francisco de Azevedo, who was shortly to follow the trail pioneered by Andrade,

> is one of those kingdoms that are classed together under the name of Pot, and it is not the smallest but rather one of the largest and richest. About a thousand years ago it was ruled over by a king called Chopado, 'the giver of the book,' because it was he who brought them the law from China on the other side of Utsang [northern Tibet]. Hence he was held in such high honour by the neighboring princes that they considered it a privilege to become allied to his family.

Azevedo is broadly correct. Buddhism flourished in Tibet from the end of the eighth century, but there was a decline in the tenth, when the Tibetan empire broke up into regional kingdoms and small princedoms. Then by 1249, when Kublai Khan invited Tibetan monks to act as chaplains at his imperial court, four major monastic Orders had come into existence, each with its own distinctive spirituality and method of contemplation, while at the same time the province of Utsang became the centre of the universities.

'The town [Tsaparang],' Azevedo continues, 'contains some good dwellings, but most of the inhabitants, driven by cold, live in mountain caves, which they call "*purgos*".' Nor is he flattering about the people: 'The position of their eyes,' he says, 'is like that of the Chinese, but their faces resemble more those of the Javanese. They are not beautiful, rather they are ugly, and so dirty in their person and clothing that they may be said to live in filth from birth to death.' 'When they marry,' he observes,

the person who has negotiated the marriage and arranged everything has the right to keep the bride in his house the first night, which in fact he generally does; the next day he gives her back to her husband. ...When they divorce (which happens frequently), the husband conducts his wife back to her parents; and each holding the opposite end of a woollen thread, they pull, break the thread, and thus the separation has become an accomplished fact. Both parties go their separate ways, the father with the son, the mother with the daughter.

Andrade speaks of the ruler of Tsaparang, the capital of the kingdom of Guge, as the King of Tibet. He gives no description of the town. He notes only that it was situated on a river. However Captain Raper, visiting the place in 1812, writes that it stood

on and around the base of a steep promontory which juts out like a buttress from the plateau into the river bed. The foot of the cliff is perhaps a mile from the stream. The ruins of the city are extensive and guarded on the other side by a chain of small rounded mud forts. Terraced fields, no longer cultivated, lie round about. Near the cliff stands the Dzongpon's house, a temple with a single lama in charge, and the dwellings of four families which constitute the population of Tsaparang. The temples are in good preservation and are kept by the Dzongpon under lock and key.[2]

Andrade's arrival in Tsaparang roused considerable suspicion: the King, Tsi-Tashi-Dagga, was unable to believe that any man who was not a merchant would undertake such a journey. But after their first meeting the King's attitude softened; he and the Queen were impressed that the priest's only motive was his religious faith. And it was not long before Andrade achieved a masterstroke: the King addressed him as the Great Lama from the West. Andrade was able to show him and his courtiers a painting of the Madonna and Child, some small crosses and various religious objects, and he attempted to explain their significance. Although he knew no Tibetan, it is unlikely that he misconstrued the local rites and practices which he observed or, as the Muslim merchants had done, saw in them vestiges of a forgotten Christianity.

When a few weeks later Andrade sought permission to leave, knowing that the Mana Pass would be closed if he stayed longer, he was allowed to depart only on condition that he returned later. 'From the supplies of corn, rice, fruit, and grapes that were sent to me by order of the King,' he wrote,

> I can only conclude that Tibet is a fertile country, but then the capital is a great exception, for it is the most barren spot I ever saw. Its only produce is a little corn in those parts that are watered by the river. The people keep large flocks of sheep, goats and horses on the plain, where for miles around, with the exception of a few humid areas, no trees or plants are to be seen. It is only during three months of the year that no snow falls and sufficient grass grows to provide pasture for the flocks. Provisions are mainly imported, even figs, peaches and wine, and all of it has to come twelve days' journey, most probably from the lower and warmer valley of the Sutlej. Because of the sterility of the country Queiximir [Kashmir], merchants say that hell lies below its surface.

Andrade noted that there was also commercial intercourse between Tsaparang and China. In fact, during his short stay in Tsaparang a caravan with four hundred merchants arrived carrying principally Chinese porcelain and coarse silks. Andrade was assured that this was an annual event, but he was also told that no traders were ever allowed to settle in the town. Owing to his ignorance of the language, Andrade was able to give no more than a brief account of the religion of the Tibetans, but he observed a ceremony which was held each month to drive out evil spirits from the town; he was told also that when a father had several sons, at least one of them became a lama, 'so that every family of more than two children had to give up one, but not the eldest, to become a lama.'

As he was on the point of leaving, Andrade was given a document under the King's seal; it read as follows:

We, the king of the Kingdoms of Potente, rejoicing in the arrival in our lands of Padre Antonio Franguim [the name given to the Portuguese in India] to teach us a holy law, take him for our Chief Lama, and give him full authority to teach the holy law to our people. We shall not permit anyone to molest him in this work. And we shall issue orders that he be given a site and all the help needed to build a house of prayer. Moreover we shall give no credence to any malicious accusations of the Moors against the padres, because we know that, as they have no law, they oppose those who follow the truth. We earnestly desire the great padre [the Provincial at Goa] to send us at once the said Padre Antonio, that he may be of assistance to our peoples. Given at Chaparangue [Tsaparang].

The King also gave him a second letter under his seal, written in Persian, for the Kashmiris of Agra and Lahore who traded with the country. He asked them to do whatever the Fathers should ask and to forward their goods as if they were the King's own.

The journey was more like a royal progress. All along the road villagers provided Andrade and his party with provisions: goats, rice and butter. Several men were sent to escort them to the frontier. Three days after setting out, they were overtaken by men carrying six boxes of small but excellent figs, more than two thousand in all, rarities from towns twelve or fifteen miles from the capital, parting tokens of esteem from the King and Queen.

But on reaching Mana, Andrade was delayed by an uprising. Three rajahs, tributaries of the King, had risen in arms against him, taking advantage of a three-point invasion of Tibet by the rajah of Srinagar. One of his armies numbered twelve thousand men with eleven thousand muskets and twenty small pieces of artillery, the second twenty thousand, the third fewer.

But heavy snowstorms broke over the mountains; and because the passes forming the lines of communication were held stubbornly at every point by the Tibetans, the invasion failed. Peace was made and Andrade was back in Agra at the beginning of November 1624. From there he wrote an account of his journey, recounting the adventures of the first European of modern times to cross the Himalayan Range, the first to descend into Tibet and bring back information about the land of the living Buddha.

———◆◆◆———

Andrade did more than make good his promise to the King that he would return. In the report of his journey that he sent to the Provincial at Goa, he added a request for men to establish a permanent centre at Tsaparang. Three priests were assigned to help him; but before they arrived in Agra, Andrade, anxious not to miss the sea-son, had begun his return journey on 13 June 1625, accompanied by one of the new priests, Gonzales de Sousa, a man of thirty-six, and by his former companion, Brother Manuel Marques.

Travelling again through Kashmir, they were for a second time molested by the rajah of Srinagar, who robbed them of most of their possessions. But they duly reached Tsaparang on 28 August, ten weeks after leaving Agra. When they were at a distance of four days from the city, they found two servants of the King waiting for them with three horses, some provisions and presents. Their goods were exempted from all dues, which amounted to one-tenth of their value, a privilege never previously granted.

Now that he had other priests to help him, Andrade worked out a broad survey of the neighbouring lands by questioning merchants from China who came to Tsaparang again that year. In a forty-page letter, divided into four chapters, that he addressed to the Jesuit General in Rome, he set out everything that he had heard about the countries and kingdoms beyond the Himalayas. 'The kingdom of Potente or Tibet,' he wrote, 'comprises the kingdom of Gogue [Guge], where we are, those of Ladakh, Mariul [an old name for the southern district of Ladakh], Rudok, Utsang, and two others further to the east. Together with the great empire of Sopo [Mongolia], which borders on China on the one side and on Moscovia on the other, they form great Tartary.'

Andrade, however, appears still not to have taken into consideration the findings of Brother Bento de Goes's journey; Goes had died in northwest China in April 1608, seventeen years earlier. 'The famous Cathayo,' Andrade wrote in the same report, 'is not a separate kingdom but a large town which is called Katay, the capital of a province situated much nearer to China and which is said to be ruled by the great king of the Sopos.'

The King at Tsaparang was faithful to his undertaking to build a house and church for the Fathers. He gave Andrade a fine site next to his palace; it was sheltered from the cold winds and faced the early morning sun. The natives living on the site had their houses pulled down and were given better accommodations elsewhere. To provide the Fathers with greater privacy, the road running close to the house was diverted. The Fathers were also given a garden where they could grow flowers for the church. On Easter Day, 2 April 1626, the foundation stone of the first Christian church in Tibet was solemnly laid. Built with the help of some friendly lamas, it was dedicated to Our Lady of Hope (Esperanza). In a letter to Rome dated 15 August 1626, Andrade clearly foresaw a great future for the mission. He was now studying the language intensely and was able to hold discussions with the monks, using certain religious practices of the Tibetans, such as fasting and the repetition of prayers, to illustrate his teaching. In his search for similarities between the religions, he was anxious not to dismiss Tibetan beliefs in their totality.

It was probably sometime in the following June that the three other priests assigned to the centre arrived in Tsaparang, two Portuguese and one Frenchman, Alain de Beauchere, from Pont-à-Mousson. Andrade was now able to establish a second station at 'Rodoa, a town belonging to a petty prince whose territory borders on Tibet'. This was the distant town of Rodok at the northern base of the Trans-Himalayan Mountains, described by a nineteenth-century traveller as

> very picturesquely situated, its site covering a steep hill which stands isolated in a plain. On the top is a large palace something similar to that at Leh and several monasteries painted red. All the houses, which were in tiers, had once been whitewashed, but the colours had toned down, and with the remains of an old wall round the town, the whole effect was extremely good.

Nowhere does Andrade explain why he chose to found a centre two hundred kilometres from Tsaparang, though it is known that the presence of the 'lamas from the West' quickly became known in neighbouring kingdoms. But he does say that the King of Ladakh wished to see him, and that in the same year, 1627, the King of

Utsang (northern Tibet) sent him a *firman* or passport with a letter inviting him to his country. Although there is no indication that Andrade visited these two places, a priest writing in 1631 refers to the King of Ladakh as a great friend of Andrade. Nor is there any evidence that either he or any of his companions visited Lhasa at this time.

The only excursion Andrade mentions that he himself made was a visit in company with the King of Tsaparang to the monastery town of Totling, no more than half a day's journey away. Five hundred lamas resided there in numerous temples, and at the time of his visit some two thousand more had come from the neighbourhood to celebrate a festival. Andrade was able to study the various degrees among them: he writes that there were ten or twelve kinds of lamas differing from one another in their rites and ceremonies. They do not marry; some live in communities, others in their own houses; they wear a sleeveless garment and over it another that comes down to their feet. Their apparel is generally red, while their headgear is usually either red or yellow. At their religious celebrations they use trumpets ordinarily made of metal but sometimes from human arm or leg bones. To remind themselves of death, they wear necklaces of human bones and, just as Friar William of Rubruck had observed in 1253, they use human skulls as drinking vessels. The ordinary people do not as a rule enter the temples, which are nearly always closed; they go there on only two days of the year to attend religious feasts.

Not only during the celebrations but in ordinary conversations in the course of the day, wherever he might be he could hear the peculiar formula of a Tibetan prayer. Sven Hedin found this prayer so intricately linked with the life of the people that he could not picture in his mind the lakes and mountains of Tibet without hearing the mystic invocation 'Om mani padme hum.' Andrade was the first to make it known to the West, but even after questioning numerous lamas, he was unable to offer an interpretation of the curious call.

It was not Andrade's policy, any more than Ricci's in China, to make immediate conversions. Nevertheless, his long-term hopes for the mission were shared by his companions at Tsaparang. 'It will be one of the most successful missions that the Society of Jesus possesses,' wrote one of Andrade's companions in 1627. Although the number of Christians was small, the prospects were good. But as might have been expected, the full backing that the King gave Andrade roused the jealousy of the lamas. The Chief Lama, the King's brother, to strengthen his position, had received into his confraternity a hundred and thirty new candidates. The King feared that if he continued in this way, his brother would deprive him of all his military and then challenge his right to his throne.

Trouble erupted soon after Andrade was recalled to Goa to take up the office of Provincial. The exact date of his departure is unknown, but it was certainly before 1630. A short time later in that year a revolution broke out: the lamas of Tsaparang called on the support of the neighbouring King of Ladakh and offered him the crown of Tsaparang. The town occupied an almost impregnable position, built as it was on the lower slopes of a hill and protected by a strong outer line of walls. On an eminence above the town was an inner circle of fortifications. This stronghold, inaccessible on all sides, could be approached only by a stairway cut out from the interior of the mountain. There was a second stairway, also cut from the rock and more than four hundred metres in length, leading to two springs situated under the inner stronghold. The castle, moreover, was well victualled and had an armoury of a thousand firearms with plenty of gunpowder and ball.

Loyal supporters of the King urged him to shelter behind the impregnable walls of his fortress. The Chief Lama, however, traitorously advised him to surrender, assuring him that the King of Ladakh, after exacting tribute, would raise the month-long siege. The pact was not honoured. The King and his family were kidnapped and carried off to Leh. The entire country was overrun, and the Christians, who numbered no more than some four hundred, were singled out for retribution: many were enslaved, others shared the King's exile. But part of the Tsaparang garrison had at the last moment retreated within the castle; there they offered such a stout resistance that in the end they were allowed to withdraw with military honours to Utsang. The viceroy of Rudok, who was on a visit to Tsaparang, had also taken refuge in the castle but could not save the town from destruction. The priests' house and church were sacked, but there was no loss of life, and although two Fathers were taken prisoner to Leh they were released soon afterwards and sent back to Tsaparang.

A contemporary Tartar history makes mention of these events. The writer says that the King of Tsaparang then ruled over a part of Tibet west of Lhasa as far as the sources of the Ganges: it asserts that he became a Christian, abandoning and then seeking to destroy the ancestral faith of the Buddha; it goes on to report that he was defeated and killed in battle. But these facts do not tally with what is known for certain from Jesuit sources. Despite the manifestations of favour displayed by the King of Tsaparang towards the Jesuits, he himself did not become a Christian. Captain G. M. Young, writing on Tsaparang in 1919, states that he did. But had the King done so, Andrade and the others with him would certainly have mentioned his conversion. Fr Francisco de Azevedo, who was in Tsaparang shortly after the revolution, goes only so far as to say that the King was inclined towards Christianity and had even promised to receive baptism but was prevented by an illicit marital union from taking the step.[3]

On 14 February 1631 Andrade, back in Goa and still unaware of the course of events in Tsaparang, sent three men to join the priests there. When the news of the upheavals reached him, Andrade, acting now as Provincial, sent Fr Francisco de Azevedo to report on the situation. Overtaking the three recruits at Agra, he ordered them to stay there to await further instructions. Leaving Agra on 28 June 1631 with Brother Marques as his companion, Azevedo set out for Tsaparang.

—◆◆◆—

Fr Azevedo's journal of his visit is one of the most fascinating accounts of Tibet dating back to this period.

Born in Lisbon in 1578, Francisco de Azevedo left for India when he was a boy and entered the Jesuit novitiate at Goa at the age of nineteen. He had worked as a priest in several stations in India before he was appointed Visitor to the mission in Mozambique. A letter of his dated 20 December 1623 is extant, reporting on the conditions of various settlements along the Cuama River. He was fifty-two, an advanced age for the task, when he left India for Tsaparang. His account of his visit fills forty-four closely written pages; parts of it have already been used to fill out Andrade's printed journal.

Azevedo wrote in a vivid style. His description of the Tibetan landscape becomes at times poetic. His pages are full of original metaphors, striking brush strokes, small details that fascinated him, and brief pen portraits. He describes as well as anyone after him the vast solitudes inhabited only by hares, wild pigeons, huge crows, eagles, horses, wild mules and yaks; once he stood on a mountain summit that dominated the Tibetan plateau; looking down upon a monastery surrounded by farmers' houses, he compared the sight to a city encircled by cribs. But he was also a man of sound practical sense.

On arriving at Srinagar, Azevedo witnessed a truly barbaric spectacle. The rajah of Garhwal, who earlier had tried to frustrate Andrade's entry into Tibet, had died. In the manner of a royal Hindu funeral, his body was laid on a large pyre of aromatic materials, chiefly aloe and precious sandalwood, and burnt on the banks of the Alaknanda. Sixty of his wives had to follow their lord onto the flames; though some did so voluntarily, most had to be thrown onto the pyre by brute force. It was not until seven days after the ceremony that the new king, a boy of seven, could be crowned.

Anxious not to delay, Azevedo was about to continue his journey when Manuel Marques, Andrade's former companion, arrived from Mana to obtain provisions for the beleaguered mission. Azevedo then learned about the revolution that had deposed the King of Tsaparang. Undeterred by all he heard, Azevedo continued his journey with Marques as his guide. Leaving Srinagar on 31 July, they took the mountain road along the river Alaknanda and reached the village of Jussy (or Josimath). Although this track had been taken by other priests, Azevedo throughout his journal adds a great deal to their accounts. 'This village,' he writes of Jussy,

is situated on the slope of a famous mountain; the houses are well built and its population numerous. The place owes its fame to a large pagoda flanked by four towers of hewn sandstone. In front of the main entrance of the pagoda the statue of an angel [*anjo*] made of bronze stands on a pedestal about three metres high. It is splendid and most artistic, particularly the features of the statue: it looks towards the pagoda in a kneeling position with hands raised to heaven.

Captain F.V. Raper, who visited this place in 1807, mentions this temple situated on the higher part of the village in a large open space where the pilgrims passed the night. In Raper's time it was surrounded by a wall about thirty feet square. At each angle and at the centre of each face were smaller temples in honour of different deities. Both the main temple and the others had been either destroyed or partially ruined by an earthquake, and there was no sign of the large statue described by Azevedo.

Continuing on his journey, Azevedo reached Mana; he found it a wretched hamlet, its people subsisting on their sheep, which they used also as beasts of burden to carry rice into Tibet and bring back loads of salt. In the neighbouring woods roved musk deer from which they obtained 'the purest and most precious milk that is known'. Here Marques was left behind: the sheep he had hired to carry provisions to the priests in Tsaparang had not yet been assembled. Azevedo therefore set out alone crossing the Mana Pass, which he described as vividly as Andrade had done.

At Tsaparang Azevedo found the Fathers and their small Christian community in a forlorn state. The King of Ladakh had taken the ruler of the country back as a prisoner to his capital Leh, after handing the town over to a governor who was hostile to the Jesuits and stationing a garrison there. Without hesitation Azevedo decided boldly to go on to Leh and treat with the King of Ladakh in person. But before setting out he made himself familiar with Tibetan etiquette. 'They never visit,' he wrote,

> without offering a present; not even a letter is sent without its accompanying gift. The host on his side must provide his guest with food and drink as often as he needs them. Anyone wishing to plead a case before the King must offer him a gift along with his petition; if his petition is granted, the gift is returned. The King on his part offers the plaintiff food, and it would be rude not to take home anything that might be left over.

As Azevedo was about to leave for Leh there was an outbreak of smallpox in Tsaparang. Fearing that Azevedo might spread the infection, the governor refused him a permit to travel. But he was won over with presents. After barely three days on the road Azevedo was overtaken by a runner with an order for him to return immediately under pain of execution. Azevedo obeyed. It was now well into September and the season for travel almost over. On 28

September he was told that within a few days he would be allowed to start afresh with some horse traders from Utsang. Choosing a priest from the centre as his companion and interpreter, he set out again for Leh on 4 October.

This was the first time a European had undertaken the journey to Leh. Travelling from sunrise to sunset, Azevedo completed the journey in twenty days. The route, which was seldom used, ran through snow-covered mountains. Not a green leaf or plant was to be seen, only an abundance of wild animals, such as hares, mountain goats, donkeys, yaks (he calls them *hyacas*), ravens and eagles. The traders had chosen this route rather than the road towards the valley of the Indus because it was practicable for horses. The track, rugged and irregular, led across the plateau between the Zaskar and Ladakh Ranges. Captain C.U. Rawlings, who crossed this plateau in 1905, speaks of the deathlike silence brooding over it, the clefts and chasms many hundred feet in depth, its spirelike pinnacles, all making a 'weird and wonderful sight, but also a depressing one. . . . Now and again in the centre of the largest *nullahs* a small crystal stream may be seen trickling over its sandy bed, but during the winter these are few and far between.'[4]

Making its way through troughs and ravines, the caravan came to Sanze (the present Shangtse), built for the greater part along the slopes of a mountain. The inhabitants, Azevedo observed, lived largely in the recesses and caves of the mountain side. Although houses were to be found, the caves were by far the more popular dwelling places. After passing another small settlement and an encampment of shepherds, they crossed 'great mountain ranges deeply covered with snow, a desert region without any settlement, until at last after seven days we reached Alner, where the chief of the lamas lives on top of a mountain. It consists of only six or seven houses which form something like a fortification.' Though the name of the place is not found on maps, it was almost certainly Hanle. An English traveller, Thomas Thomson, found a Buddhist monastery there in 1847 built on the summit of a steep hill rising abruptly from the plain. It was then the home of some twenty lamas, one of the highest inhabited places on earth.

From Hanle the caravan made its way across a bare plateau; then passing along some sheltered valleys, it came upon another shepherds' encampment of some thirty tents. Azevedo speaks here of eighteen or twenty thousand sheep that found pasture on the borders of small rivers. The shepherds gave the priests milk in return for three raisins the size of plums which they had brought with them from Hindustan.

The next three days were spent once more among barren mountains. 'We were half-dead with cold,' says Azevedo, whose face and hands were all chapped, with blood running down them. Even the guards were affected; there was no firewood to be had, not even dung. Towards evening on the third day they saw a wide valley opening up ahead of them in which there was a large salt marsh with fine white salt. After stopping here for the night, they resumed their journey through the mountains for another three days until they came to the town of Gya, the third and last place name mentioned by Azevedo between Tsaparang and Leh.

Gya was described by a nineteenth-century traveller as a 'town of small extent and thinly populated', some forty houses with a wide cultivated area. At the time of the priests' visit, it had a governor installed by the King of Ladakh; he welcomed them warmly and among other presents gave them twelve large apples 'much resembling,' writes Azevedo, 'the very large and good ones of Lisbon' that he had not seen for thirty-seven years. Rested and refreshed, the party resumed the trek to Leh.

'After two days we arrived at a station in the kingdom of Ladakh,' the journal continues,

> from where six small hamlets can be seen at a mile's distance from each other. . . . They lie in the widest and longest valley I have seen in those mountain regions and which also contains many fertile fields of barley. The barley is not like that of our country; its grain resembles more that of wheat, but as food it is very nourishing and pleasant to the taste. The next day we reached the royal town of Lee [Leh], the capital of the kingdom of Ladakh.

It was the evening of 25 October 1631. Azevedo and his companion were the first Europeans to enter Leh, but before they could do so, they first had to comply with certain formalities. As they approached the town they had to dismount and stand waiting for permission to enter. When it was eventually given, they were escorted to lodgings assigned to them by the King and were provided with fuel, water and some measures of barley. 'Leh,' writes Azevedo, 'is built on the slope of a small mountain and numbers about eight hundred families. About half a mile further down but still quite visible flows the river that goes to Lahore. A mountain stream passes through the town itself and works a large number of water mills; there are also a few trees.'

Azevedo gives the boundaries of Ladakh: 'The kingdom of Ladakh,' he writes,

> borders in the south on that of Chaparangue or Guge, in the east on the kingdom of three Moors, also called by another name, Archande [Yarkand], the capital of which is Cascar [Kashgar]. It is from there that caravans carry into China the clay of which porcelain is made. Through this kingdom, with its curiously white and strongly built population, Brother Bento de Goes travelled. Cascar is not more than six days' march from the kingdom of Ladakh. On the western side, finally, it is bounded by the kingdom of Baldys [Baltistan], whose people are not so white but are taller and have a better physique.

The very first day after their arrival, the King had the strangers sent for. He did not want so much to see them in person, writes Azevedo, as to receive their presents: they consisted of some pieces of cloth, six large and six small firearms, two Chinese targets, an inkstand from Diu and some other gilt trinkets, all of which were eagerly accepted. Azevedo sketches a vivid portrait of the King, Senge-Namgyal, the accuracy of which is confirmed by the chronicles, describing him as

> a man of tall stature, of a brown colour, with something of the Javanese in his features, and of stern appearance. He wore a rather dirty upper garment of some red material, a mantle of the same stuff and a threadbare cap. His hair hung down his shoulders, both ears were adorned with turquoise and a large coral, and he wore a string of skull bones round his neck to remind himself of death. He was sitting cross-legged on an ornamental carpet of crimson velvet dating from the time of Methuselah.

The Queen, a short, stout person with sore eyes, was dressed like her husband but was less imposing. When everyone was seated, Chinese tea was served, a sign of great favour on the King's part. The tea was made with water, some butter and a little milk: a dark liquid drunk as hot as possible. 'One who serves tea,' Azevedo continues, 'is reputed a very generous host, but on account of the cost only the rich can do so.' After this ceremony the Fathers were presented with a piece of raw meat and a ball of husked barley called *zanem*. Finally, most of those present accompanied the priests back to their residence.

For the rest of their stay, the Fathers, who could not afford the expensive tea, made do with barley meal, either baked into a sort of pancake or kneaded into dough and rolled into balls that could be packed conveniently when travelling.

All that Azevedo has to say about the palace is that it was full of cobwebs; the chronicles, however, describe how the nine-storey building was constructed and report that it was completed about nine years before the priests arrived.

During his first audience, which had been primarily a formal greeting, Azevedo had not touched on the reason for his coming. Four days later, in his second interview, he had a chance to submit his proposals to the King, who undertook to consider them with his councillors. Then a week later the King sent the priests his decision: the priests could continue their work in places where they had begun in the reign of the late king, not only in the kingdom of Coge, but also in Ridocho, and even in Leh itself. At the same time he presented Azevedo with a horse, four pieces of woollen stuff and two yak's tails; he also granted him permission to leave.

Azevedo had not planned to stay any length of time in Leh. He was anxious to return to Agra to report on the situation in Tibet. Setting out again with his companion in intense cold, he arrived just three days later at Gya. It was 10 November 1631. Here he consulted the local authorities and decided to leave at once even though the cold had grown still more intense. There were eighteen stages on the road between Gya and Tsaparang. The Mana Range had to be crossed: although this was not impossible in winter, it could only be done with imminent risk. 'But if I took the direct road to Lahore,' Azevedo reflected, 'it would, it is true, be a new route across uninhabited regions and through numerous petty king-doms, but it had this great advantage that after nine days we would have escaped the terrible winter. In the end, I resolved to take this new route to Lahore so that I should not have to spend the winter in Chaparangue [Tsaparang].'

Accordingly, the very day of their arrival at Gya, the two priests took leave of the ruler. He entreated them to return with one or more priests and promised to build them a house and to support them.

Although the priests took with them an experienced guide, their courage was not the less remarkable: they were setting out ill-equipped in the most unfavourable season of the year on a journey across the uninhabited plateaus of Rupshu and Lahul and over Himalayan passes dangerous enough in fine weather.

This was the old trade route that ran and still runs from Yarkand via Leh to the Punjab. Though regularly used by the native population, it had never been taken by Europeans. It was only a hundred and ninety years later that an Englishman, William Moorcroft, penetrated into this region of the Himalayas: in winter the snow-storms swirled through the valleys, obstructed the passes and concealed the tracks. Several times the priests were in danger of their lives. 'For nine days,' writes Azevedo,

> we travelled through a solitude of plateaus and moun-
> tain ranges without meeting a soul. Crossing frozen
> streams and rivers, we arrived at a place where
> numerous springs issue from the mountains, their
> water freezing as it comes out. On the slope of one
> mountain, I counted, within the distance of a gunshot,
> one hundred and twenty-seven springs, but there was
> not a single blade of grass to be seen. We experienced
> the greatest difficulty in those wastes when we
> climbed and came down from a very steep mountain
> that was completely covered with snow and, in some
> places, with ice: it took us an entire day with the snow
> reaching above our knees; no road was visible and we
> fell, got up again, slipped on the ice: it was difficult to
> keep or regain a foothold. Thank God there was plenty
> of sunshine and no wind that day or we would have
> been frozen to death. On the summit of this great
> mountain. . . . there was one huge sheet of ice glitter-
> ing in the sun with a brilliance that blinded the eye.

This was the mountain marked Lachalung on the maps. Two days after coming down from its frozen summit, Azevedo and his companions made their way through the Bhaga Valley in the face of an ice storm so fierce that they almost froze to death. Azevedo writes that he was so numbed that he had to be lifted from his horse and revived. The evening of that day was spent over a fire in a cave by a frozen stream, where they ate a few pieces of black bran bread, 'blacker than the blackest bread that can be found', and some barley-meal porridge.

The next day, the ninth after leaving Gya, the cold was less severe. Towards eleven in the morning they saw four cypress trees on a river bank; continuing on their way, they came across more trees and numerous clear springs. Then about four in the afternoon they entered the first settlement of the little kingdom of Carja or Caria. In the house of a lama the party was given toasted bread and milk. The next morning they continued in the direction of the kingdom of Culu (Kulu).

Here the road ran between two mountain ranges covered with trees and vegetation. They passed through a number of small villages where the people lived by agriculture and cattle breeding: Azevedo found them finely built, kindly disposed and much cleaner than the Tibetans. But the lateness of the season caused fresh difficulties. On the frontier of Lahul, the snowfall was so heavy that they were constantly losing their way.

Soaked to the skin, they arrived numbed at the foot of a mountain and passed the night there in the shelter of a cave. Azevedo's boots, not made for mountaineering, were worn through. Unwilling to climb the mountain in such weather, they rested for two nights. On the third day, after Azevedo had obtained a pair of shoes made of twisted straw, they began the ascent. The horses sank up to their bellies in the snow. 'I shoved myself along with the greatest difficulty,' Azevedo recalls, 'without being able to take any rest, for if I stopped for a moment I sank into the snow up to my chest.' For five hours he struggled on. Then his strength failed before he could reach the summit. He thought he would die there. It was only with the help of his guide and companions (some Lahulis had joined the party that morning) that he survived, carried in their arms. Unable to reach the foot of the mountain that night the party camped on the downward slope looking down with longing on the magnificent cedars in the valley below. They were on the Rotang Pass connecting Lahul and Kulu. A.F.P. Harcourt states that in 1963, of the hundred labourers who crossed the mountain during a storm, seventy-two died. 'I shall long remember that day,' wrote Azevedo, 'because my hands, which I sprained several times in my repeated falls, have remained partly deformed.'

After another three days they reached Nagar, the capital of the kingdom of Kulu, set in a mountain valley with numerous cedars. Azevedo remarked on the fine features of the people, on the charming children with golden hair and some women who were as white as the Portuguese; he saw some fine and very comfortable houses with roofs and verandahs made of cedar wood, and thought it strange that all the people wore flowers or odoriferous herbs in their headgear. The king was absent at the time, but a kinsman of his, who had at first received Azevedo kindly, deprived him of his horse and a few small items. 'But I let things be,' Azevedo wrote, 'so that I could have his permission to continue my journey.'

The two priests were the first Europeans to cross this delightful region of the Himalayas, which is said to rival Kashmir for beauty of scenery. In the four days' march that took them to the kingdom of Mandi they ran short of provisions. When Azevedo was still in Tsaparang, he had gathered a supply of herbs that he calls naruleys, a sort of root plant that was thought to have medicinal properties against fever and other ailments. These he was able to exchange for provisions. Although the going was now easy, Azevedo's feet suffered so badly that he could walk only with difficulty and none of the party was prepared to carry him any further. So for the rest of the journey to Mandi he was made to sit in a 'gemary', carried by four bearers.

At Mandi, a tributary state of the Mogul, Azevedo encountered fanatical hatred from some Muslims, while the governor robbed them of everything he considered worth stealing. Then after crossing the last spur of the Himalayas, they left the mountains behind. 'I had spent five months without seeing much more than snow,' he remarked in his journal.

He now changed his plan. Instead of going on to Lahore, he made for Delhi. From there he made his way to Agra, his starting point. He arrived there on 3 January 1632, six months and five days after setting out.

But because of intermittent civil war, the priests in Tsaparang were unable to make any progress. Little news from Tsaparang came through to Agra. On 6 February 1633 one of the priests there wrote: 'Three days ago we received letters from the mission in Tibet. The five Fathers who are there tell us that they are like prisoners in their own house. The commander does not allow them to return here or to leave the place where they now are or to carry anything out of the house without his seeing it.' The following October further news came: there had been no change in the situation. The Fathers were still virtual prisoners in Tsaparang. All the other stations had been overrun by war.

As soon as his term of office as Provincial was over, Andrade decided to return to Tibet himself. Six others were to go with him, but while he was preparing to set out, he died suddenly on 19 March 1634. Consequently, the expedition was postponed to the beginning of 1635. 'Of my six companions,' wrote Nuno Coresma, a young Spaniard from the district of Tordesillas, the leader of the party, 'only one reached Chaparangue [Tsaparang] with me. Two died on the way, and the other three became so ill that it would have been inhuman to have taken them further and have them die in this desolate country.' The three therefore were left behind at Srinagar. 'The snow was up to our knees,' reported Coresma, and in many places up to the waist, and a cold, numbing wind was blowing. The war has ravaged the country. The population is very small, as can be seen from the fact that in the whole of the territory, which for lack of knowledge has been called Cathay, it is impossible to assemble two thousand warriors, although all are bound to serve from their eighteenth to their eightieth year. In this town [Tsaparang], which is the mercantile emporium of the whole country, it is impossible to find more than five hundred inhabitants, including a hundred who are slaves of the rajah. The people are very poor, uncivilized and rude. . . . they live on a little roasted barley pounded into a meal, take some raw meat only occasionally and drink one or two bowls of tea a day.

The governor appointed by the King of Ladakh was unfriendly and did nothing to stop the people from constantly hurling stones at the Fathers' house. Moreover, it was difficult to supply the missions. 'The country is mostly dry and barren,' Coresma explained, 'very mountainous and sparsely populated. There is a complete lack of trees, not just fruit trees but trees for firewood. There are no herbs, only a little barley and corn which is very stunted because the fields are not tilled.' It was impossible to get supplies from Hindustan or Srinagar, for a quantity of rice purchased for one rupee at Srinagar sold at Tsaparang for ten or twelve times as much.

The number of Christians had shrunk; the few who remained were scattered in different places. The sacrifices that had already been made and those that would be required to maintain the missions seemed out of proportion to the scanty results. The King of Ladakh, on whose support the centre depended, had done nothing to make good his promise of assistance. The situation worsened yearly. In 1634 the guard over the remaining Jesuits in Tsaparang was strengthened. All communication with the outside world was cut. Finally, in December the mission in Tsaparang was formally abandoned. In 1919 a British officer, Captain G.M. Young, published an account of his visit to Tsaparang. He examined every building around the King's palace. 'I entered every house in the city that I could,' he wrote,

> but found no trace of a church or a mission. Most of the houses are amazingly well preserved, although the roof timbers have been taken long ago for fuel, except from the temples. The lamas no doubt abolished the mission buildings just as thoroughly as they wiped out the King's name from their chronicles. Judging by Andrade's account, the church must have been somewhere near what is now the Dzongpon's house. The inhabitants profess, truthfully, I dare say, to have no tradition whatever of the Jesuits or of the King's conversion.[5]

In 1944 two young prisoners of war escaping into Tibet from an internment camp in northern India passed through Tsaparang. 'Tsaparang,' writes one of them, Heinrich Harrer (an Austrian),

> was a real curiosity. I had learned from the books I had studied in the camp that the first Catholic mission station in Tibet had been established here in 1624. The

Portuguese Jesuit Antonio de Andrade had formed a
Catholic community and is said to have built a church.
We searched for traces of it, but could not find any
remains. Our own experience made us realize how
difficult it must have been for Fr Antonio to establish
his mission here.[6]

[1]F.V. Raper, 'Narrative of a Survey for the purpose of discovering
the Sources of the Ganges' in *Asiatic Researches Transactions*, vol. XI
(London, 1812), 531.
[2]Ibid., 536.
[3]G.M. Young, 'A Journey to Toling and Tsaparang in Western Tibet'
in the *Journal of the Punjab Historical Society*, vol. VII (Calcutta, 1919),
198.
[4]C.G. Rawlings, *The Great Plateau, being an account of exploration in
central Tibet* (London, 1904), 281.
[5]Young, op. cit., 196.
[6]Heinrich Harrer, *Seven Years in Tibet* (London, 1953), 30.

Estevão Cacella and João Cabral

During his second stay at Tsaparang in 1625 Antonio de Andrade had questioned merchants coming from China and gathered all the information he could get about the extent of Tibet. He learned that it was a vast country, known to the merchants as Utsang, and that it was situated one and a half months' journey from his base at Tsaparing. Beyond it lay Cathay. Even then, Goes's insistence that this country was identical with China was not universally accepted.

Here in Utsang and beyond in Cathay was a new field for missionary exploration. Accordingly, Andrade wrote to his Superior in Cochin, southern India, proposing that an attempt should be made to reach these unknown easterly regions via Bengal. The suggestion was duly acted upon, and early in 1626 two Portuguese Jesuits, Estevão Cacella and João Cabral, were chosen for the venture.

Cacella came from Aviz in the diocese of Évora. Having joined the Jesuits at the age of nineteen, he had sailed for India in 1614. On completing his studies he had worked for some years in Kerala in southeastern India. The man assigned to accompany him, Cabral, was fourteen years younger. A native of Celorico in the province of Beira, he had entered the Society in 1615, a year after Cacella had sailed from Lisbon.

On 30 April 1626 the two Portuguese priests departed from Cochin together with a Brother, Bartolomeo Fonteboa, a native of Florence, then fifty years old. Fonteboa had served as an artist in Bandraginore and elsewhere and had already some experience of Bengal to his credit. With him as their guide on the first leg of their journey the Fathers set out for Utsang. From there they hoped to find their way to Cathay.

Cabral later wrote a long record of their adventures, which was sent on to Rome after it had first been read, presumably in Portuguese, some time before 1635 to the Jesuit students in their house of studies in Coimbra. It has since been lost. However, both Cacella and Cabral wrote two long letters in the course of their journey that form the basis of this account.

After two and a half months on the road, the party arrived on 10 July at Hugli on the Ganges Delta, where the Jesuits had a mission. Cacella was sanguine. The road to Cathay, he reported back to Cochin, was much frequented; it offered no serious obstacles and the people there were said to behave like Christians. He intended, therefore, to journey to Cocho by way of Siripur, where he had hopes of meeting Cathayan traders whom he could join in October on their return journey to their country. He would write again from Cocho.

Leaving Hugli on 2 August and taking with them Fr Simon de Figueiredo from the mission to act as their guide, the party, which now numbered four, set out for Siripur and Dacca. They had disguised themselves as Portuguese soldiers, for Dacca was then governed by Muslims in the absence of the Nawab, who was at Rajamahal, in his palace on the Ganges opposite Maldah Town, the ancient seat of the government of Bengal before it was transferred to Dacca about 1610. On reaching Siripur, Cacella, the head of the expedition, left his companion Cabral behind and went ahead to reconnoitre with Simon de Figueiredo. When they arrived at Dacca, the two priests were arrested and imprisoned: their fears of the Muslim regime had proved well founded. However, after twelve days they were released and Cacella was able to send a boat down to Siripur to fetch Cabral. Because of the threat of further difficulties, they sent the Brother, Bartholomeo Fonteboa, back to the Jesuit house at Hugli. A man of fifty and in poor health at the time, Fonteboa died at Hugli on 26 December the same year.

On 5 September Cacella and Cabral resumed their journey by river. Passing some sixty *choquins* or custom-houses on the way, they reached Azo (Hajo) just three weeks later. 'Azo,' wrote Cabral,

is a most important town and the capital of the kingdom of Cocho, a large country and very populous and rich. It used to be the residence of Liquinarane, king of Cocho, who is now dead: the nababo of Mogor, to whom the country pays tribute, also resides there. We passed the town and arrived at Pando [Paro], where lives Satargit, rajah of Busna, the pagan commander-in-chief of Mogor in the war against the Assames. Pando does not cover a very large territory, but it is densely populated. It stretches no great

distance into the interior but extends along the beautiful River Cocho, which is the cause of the war they are
constantly waging against the Assames, their neigh-
bours.

On their arrival at Paro, the priests were welcomed by Rajah
Satargit, the commander-in-chief. They explained their intention
of going on to Utsang and Cathay. The rajah was baffled. After
making enquiries, he told the priests that none of his people had
ever heard of Cathay. 'There was no one who had any knowledge
of the country,' he said,

> except a Moor, who told us that it lay beyond a town
> called Cascar [Kashgar], through which one passes
> into that country. He knew of no road leading to it
> from Cocho, but we were sure to find one after cross-
> ing the mountains of Potente [Tibet]. When we asked
> how we were to get into the kingdom of Potente,
> Satargit proposed that we should consult Liquinarane,
> the king of Cocho, at Azo: the King was well acquaint-
> ed with that people: they came down into his country
> from the mountains.

Satargit himself conducted the travellers back to Azo (Hajo), a
town described by an English explorer, W. Griffith, in 1837 as a
place of considerable note. At the time of Cacella's visit, it was situated on the river Brahmaputra, but before Griffith's visit the river
had shifted its course some way southward, close to some low hills.
The courtesy of the rajah impressed Cacella, who praises him
lavishly for his kindness. 'Thanks to his knowledge and to his position,' Cacella writes, 'his prestige is great throughout the country,
as we noted in Azo, where the people in the streets cheered him as
if he were their sovereign. This also is in part due to his great liber-
ality in disposing of his income, which amounts to about 200,000
tangas.' However, not very long after the visit of the priests,
Satargit quarrelled with the governors of Bengal, made common
cause with Assam against his own sovereign, and was subse-
quently captured and executed.

On entering the palace at Azo but before they could obtain access
to Liquinarane, the king of Cocho, the travellers had to pass
through three courts enclosed by roomy verandahs and separated
from each other by strong gates. Passing the third gate, they

entered a large garden, in the middle of which stood a villa where the King awaited them. The King received the priests kindly, listened to their plans, and advised them to take the road to Behar, where his son, Gaburrasa, was ruler. From there they could proceed to Runate, the furthest part of his dominions, and thence to Potente or Tibet. The King then gave them letters to his son at Behar, and both he and the rajah liberally provided for their travelling expenses.

Leaving Azo thirteen days later, Cacella and Cabral reached Behar (Cooch Behar) on 21 October of the same year. They were not the first Europeans to visit the town: a London merchant named Ralph Fitch had been there before them as early as 1586. 'I went from Bengala,' Fitch wrote,

> into the countrie of Couche which lieth five and twenty days' journey northward from Tanda. The King is a gentile, his name is Suckel Counse [Shuki Gossain]; his country is great and lieth not far from Cauchin China, for they say they have pepper from thence. The port is called Cacchogate [Chichakota], north of the town of Cooch Behar in the Bengal Duars. . . . Here they have much silk and musk and cloth made of cotton. The people have ears that be marvellous great of a span long which they draw out in length when they be young. Here they be all gentiles and they kill nothing.[1]

Cacella adds some details to this description by Fitch. Like the English merchant, he too noted that it was a very populous place with many bazaars and was famous for its fruit, which he judged 'better here than he had seen in India and especially its oranges of every kind'.

On their arrival at Cooch Behar on 21 October, the priests learned to their disappointment that the king, Gaburrasa, had deserted the town. He had moved to the interior in order to escape the floods that had devastated his capital, and had taken up residence at a place called Colambarim on a tributary of the same river. The merchants had followed him and already a new town was taking shape with larger and more regular streets. This new town, which would have been somewhere near Cooch Behar, is not found on maps. Cacella does not say when the move was made, but it was not uncommon for royalty to move their residences from time to time. Fitch notes that the houses were built on staves so that the flood waters could pass underneath them.

Thanks to their letters of introduction, the priests were well received by the King. In the market they made enquiries of some eight natives of Potente (Tibet) and were told that the snows made it impossible to cross the mountains in winter. Try as they might, they could find no one to conduct them any further. They now had to remain in the kingdom of Cocho for four months. There was not a single person who had heard of a country named Tibet. A Persian whom they met thought that beyond the mountains there were two vast countries, one of which was called O, the other Uturum. The town of Runate marked the farthest extent of the kingdom of Cocho; beyond that began the country of Botente (Potente), which stretched very far, even beyond Nepal.

The two priests returned therefore to Behar. They then sent their interpreter with letters back to Hugli, instructing him to bring Brother Fonteboa with him on his return, so that the Brother could be with them in their journey to Potente. They were unaware that Fonteboa had died the previous December. In the damp and malarial climate of Behar, the two priests were struck down with a violent fever, and almost at the same time their servant boys were taken ill. Cacella recovered fairly quickly; but owing to the almost total absence of proper care, Cabral and the boys hovered for a long time close to death. All through November and December Cabral's condition remained critical.

However, on 2 February 1627, carrying letters for the governor of Runate and the people of Potente, the two priests set out from Behar in order to make preparations at Runate for their journey over the mountains. At Runate, tired of waiting for the return of their messenger from Hugli, they decided to go ahead without him, but on 21 February, as they were on the point of departure, he returned with news of Fonteboa's death.

After four days spent crossing a mountain range (the present border between Bengal and Bhutan), following the caravan trail to Gyantse and on to Shigatse, Cacella and Cabral arrived at the first village of the new country. At once they encountered difficulties. During their stay in Runate, they had been befriended by an unnamed person of position who happened to be there on business.

He had not accompanied the priests himself but had sent his servants on ahead with them with instructions to retain them in the village until he himself arrived six months later.

As the villagers refused to give the priests help of any kind, they were virtually prisoners. After trying for twelve days to come to terms with the villagers, Cacella resolved to go ahead without their consent. Leaving Cabral behind and undaunted by descriptions of the dangers of the road ahead, he set out, taking with him only a Christian boy and two men from Cocho who had a smattering of the language. On their way they met two soldiers, who told them they were making for the same country. But the following day, as they were crossing a mountain stream, the soldiers, making common cause with the two men from Cocho, robbed Cacella of all his possessions. Left now with only the Christian boy, without a guide and without any knowledge of the language, Cacella began to retrace his steps. On a dark night, while making his way in a heavy fall of snow, he crept on all fours along the narrow mountain paths. In recounting his story later, he says that he was fortunate that his worthy travelling companions had left him with nothing more than his walking stick and breviary. On his return he found that Cabral had managed to negotiate his release.

On 16 March they set out again together and after six days in the mountains they arrived at another village, now impossible to identify, called Rintan. Here the regional king had a house in which they were entertained. They moved on from there and four days later came to Pargao, the present-day town of Paro, on 25 March 'It lies in a beautiful, wide plain,' writes Cacella,

> which extends very pleasantly between two mountain ranges. At that time the fields were covered with promising crops of wheat and rice. Two rivers divide the plain and lend it freshness and beauty, especially thanks to large willow trees and the numerous irrigation canals that are connected with the rivers. The houses begin at the very edge of the plain. They are large, high buildings, usually of four or five storeys, with very thick walls adorned with windows and verandahs: these houses form a town of such length that the part of it which we saw and crossed must be at least three leagues, and there was another part we

did not see. For the plain continues in the way I have said until it comes to a mountain ridge that splits it lengthwise. . . . I estimate that about 500,000 souls are living there. This is because they divide these houses into different stories and tenements.

It is likely that Cacella and Cabral were the first Europeans to enter this region. Ralph Fitch had heard of it but had not been there himself: he had been told that its people were 'tall and strong and that there are merchants there that come out of China and they say out of Muscovia and Tartarie also.'[2] It was not until 1777 that another European penetrated so far north. That year a magistrate, George Bogle, and Dr A. Hamilton of the Indian Medical Service went through Bhutan dispatched by Warren Hastings, then governor of Bengal, with the aim of establishing trade relations with western Tibet. Hastings, who was principally responsible for converting the East India Company into a sovereign power, followed this up with a second mission in 1783. Both failed to reach Lhasa or to obtain any commercial treaty because of the hostility of the Chinese Resident in the capital.

On their arrival at Paro, the priests received the same kind of rough handling they had experienced after crossing the frontier: they were locked up, robbed of everything they had, and told to await the arrival of the same man who had tried to obstruct their journey earlier. After two days, however, the priests noticed that no strict guard was kept and decided to walk out of their prison. But a violent mob gathered around them, threatening them with weapons. Cacella stood unmoved. He declared that he was going straight to their king. His intrepidity impressed the crowd and it soon dispersed. On 5 April, Easter Sunday, Cacella and Cabral resumed their journey. After crossing some high mountains, they drew near to the place where the King happened to be living at the time. The King had been told of their coming and had prepared a warm welcome.

On their third day out they were met by a lama bringing them servants and also horses for them all to ride the short remaining distance. Then came a second messenger with two beautifully caparisoned horses for the two Fathers. Then a little further on they were brought tea, a favourite beverage of the King and his attendants. And finally they were met by a group of young lamas on horseback who engaged in horse races as they came down to the plain. 'Immediately after this,' writes Cacella,

> we discovered among the trees a large crowd waiting for us. Then there was a burst of music from instruments resembling clarions and trumpets. A hundred young lamas, from twelve to twenty years old, came out in double file to greet us while three smaller ones walked in the middle carrying burning perfumes, which is a homage to royalty. In this way we were conducted to our lodgings, a well-made tent lined with Chinese silk and adorned with a canopy. After a short interval we were summoned to the King's presence and ushered into another tent which was also richly ornamented with silks.
>
> The King was seated on a dais draped with red silk and embroidered with gold. Close to him, on his right, on a similar platform, stood a statue of his father, in front of which a lamp was kept burning. There were also two raised seats for us, while all the lamas, whatever their rank, sat on the mats that covered the floor. The reception was very warm; and in reply to the usual questions as to where we came from and who we were, I told him that we were Portuguese, for the name Franguis by which the Portuguese are known throughout the East was unknown to them: foreigners, in fact, never enter these mountain regions nor can anyone remember ever having seen one or heard of their passing through the place.

The conversation was conducted through an interpreter who happened to be at the court and had some knowledge of Hindustani. The King was called Droma Rajah or Dharma Rajah. He was thirty-three and was both King and Great Lama of this realm of Cambirasi (a name not found in any map or chronicle, but which must refer to the northwestern territory of Bhutan); this was the first kingdom of Potente. The King was highly regarded both for his gentleness and his abstinence from rice, flesh and fish, living as he did on milk and fruit. Once he had spent three years in solitude in a hut on a large projecting rock on a mountain without seeing or receiving anyone. By means of two ropes he was able to haul up any food he needed to nourish himself in his almost inaccessible hermitage. Much of his time he devoted to contemplation and he spent his leisure moments carving images. He showed the visitors one of them, an image of the face of God (*'imagem de vulto de Deos'*) carved in white sandalwood, small but beautifully executed. When Cacella showed him a picture of the archangel Raphael, he wanted to make a copy of it and at once set to work on it. He had a great reputation as a scholar and had about him lamas from distant countries.

From time to time the people would invite their ruler to their districts, where he lived with the local lamas. The two priests accompanied him on his progress from one village to the next and afterwards lived with him in one of his houses, which was on the same mountain as his hermitage.

There is little in the native chronicles to set against Cacella's narrative. The Droma Rajah's capital was Rahjum (the modern Ralung), about thirty miles east of Gyantse. Rahjum had and still has a famous monastery, Dukpa, the headquarters or mother house of the Red Hat sect of lamas which reigns supreme in Bhutan. The rajah did not live there, but preferred his mountain residence, which gave him some measure of protection against a neighbouring prince who carried on an intermittent war against him. This young rajah, in his thirties at the time of the priests' visit, was in fact captured and held a prisoner in 1661 in the war against the Muslims in the Bhutan hills. A Bhutanese chronicler of that time confirms Cacella: he writes that 'he is an ascetic, eats only plantains, drinks only milk, and indulges in no pleasures whatever. He is famous for his justice and rules over a large people.'

At the rajah's court the priests were able to study the daily life of the lamas. The younger lamas, one hundred in number, who belonged to the King's retinue, formed a kind of monastic school whose chief occupation was to learn the rites and ceremonies of their religion. 'They are called Guelofs,' writes Cacella,

> and are the most important among the lamas because they do not marry and take only one meal a day, before midday; after that they are not permitted to take any rice, flesh or fish. Moreover they never drink wine and in all these ways are marked off from the other lamas who follow less strict observances. Twice

71

a day, in the morning and afternoon, they all go out in a body. A great part of the day is spent in prayer, and even during the night they rise at a given signal to pray for half an hour, which they do in the early hours, chanting after the manner of clerics in choir.

The routine of the monastery changed little in time. Samuel Turner, in an account of a journey made a hundred and fifty years later through Bhutan and parts of Tibet, writes that the monks gathered in their chapel in the morning, at noon, and at night. 'We were regularly roused at the earliest dawn,' he records, 'by the clamorous noise of numerous instruments to whose sounds they chanted their orisons.'[3] Nor had their dress changed since the visit of the two priests; moreover they still wore their hair short and still refused to carry arms.

Cacella and Cabral, however, experienced difficulties in their attempt to learn the language of the lamas. They were unable to find a good teacher. 'The one we had,' Cacella complained, 'did not know the language of these parts. . . . For although these kingdoms have the same language, there is a great deal of difference in pronunciation and endings, and in some parts of the country there are so many corruptions that it becomes almost a different language.'

However, at the time this letter was written, on 10 July 1626, the priests were able with difficulty to read the books of the lamas that were written in a polished style. Moreover, before leaving they could even compose some prayers and religious instructions in the vernacular.

Not everything Cacella reported about the religion of Bhutan is entirely accurate: he was there only a short time, and what he wrote is partially coloured by his hope of finding Christian communities in these northern regions. He was too ready to see in Buddhist practices garbled relics of the Christian faith introduced there in earlier centuries. Nevertheless, he is correct in speaking of the great reverence in which his host, Dharma Rajah, the king and great lama, was held. The rajah was offered large presents by his people, Cacella reported, so that at their death his prayers would dispatch them swiftly to heaven. 'When death draws near,' he wrote, 'the King is sent for, and at the very moment of death he pulls out some of the man's hair and in this way helps his soul to heaven. If he pulls the hair out before death, great harm would ensue.' L. A. Waddell, writing at the end of the nineteenth century, adds that after death the person's body is not disturbed until the lama has extracted the soul in the orthodox manner. For the people believe that any movement of the corpse might eject the soul, which would then wander about in an irregular manner and be seized by some demon. On death, therefore, a white cloth is thrown over the head of the corpse and the soul-extracting lama is sent for. When he arrives, all the weeping relatives and friends are sent out of the room where the body lies, the doors and windows are closed in order to secure silence and the lama then seats himself on a mat at the head of the corpse. He then begins his chants, which contain directions for the soul to find its way to the western paradise of the mythical Buddha-Amitabha. The lama then advises the spirit to quit the body and all worldly ties and property. And only when all this has been done does he take between his forefinger and thumb a few hairs from the crown of the corpse's head. By plucking them forcibly he is supposed to provide a vent for the spirit to escape and pass liberated into eternity.[4]

As elsewhere, Cacella and Cabral made inquiries about Cathay. They were told that there was a country called Xembala, but nothing was known about the religion of its people: it was a large country bordering on Tartary: that no one had heard of Cathay was regarded by the priests as of no significance, since Tartary, China and Tibet all had different names in this land: China was called Guena, Tartary Sopo, and Tibet Potente.

In spite of the rajah's kindness, it was agreed between the two priests that mission work in Paro stood little chance of success. When they made it clear that they wanted to move on to regions to the north and west, the rajah was piqued: all the country knew that they were his guests, and their departure would reflect on his hospitality; he promised to allow them to preach their Christian religion and to build them a house and church. After agreeing to stay, Cacella soon regretted his decision. But he proposed a compromise instead: Cacella would go, leaving Cabral behind provided the King made good his promise to build a house of prayer. The offer appealed to the priests for, as Cacella wrote, 'there are very few temples here. During the sixteen days of our mountain journey, we noticed just one right on top of a mountain on a protruding rock, and the only thing we saw in Paro was a lama's small house that served as a temple.' What Cacella did not realize was that no special buildings were set aside for religious devotions; the services in this region were held before altars erected in large apartments or in the palaces and castles where the Gylongs lived. The people were not obliged to attend. But by the roadsides there were small shrines, hardly temples, containing either a painted or sculptured representation of a deity. These images were similar to the small carvings that the rajah had showed to the priests: some of them were of fine craftsmanship and were thought to have been inspired by the Chinese.

Remembering no doubt how ill he had been at Behar, Cacella found that the climate at Paro suited him perfectly. 'Never in India,' he wrote on 4 October,

> did I enjoy such good health: all the people are the same. We rarely see a sick man, and there are a great number of old and elderly people who are still hale and hardy. We have been in this hill country for more than seven months and all the time the temperature has been very moderate, neither extremely hot nor cold. From November to February it is colder, but the people are well protected by woollen clothing.

The abundance of fruit would have helped to keep the priests in good health. Cacella writes enthusiastically of the plentiful pears, peaches, apples, walnuts, quinces, Indian lemons and peas. The turnips were also very good; an English traveller, Clements Markham, in 1879 declared them the best in the world.[5] Grapes, however, were not grown but were brought in from places like Congpo, a Tibetan province on the border of Kham, some twenty miles away. The people traded also with Kashmir, Gyangtse, and Lhasa; in fact it appeared an ideal centre for the priests to establish a mission. 'But to the hill country, where we live,' writes Cacella,

> no stranger even turns his steps, and the only thing the people here can recollect is the rare passage of some jogue or other. Nor does anyone come here from Cocho except the slaves, who are obtained from here. When some years ago an uncle of the King of Cocho, either from curiosity or from love of travelling, entered these mountainous districts, he was caught after

a few days on the road and put to the plough. When
the King of Cocho got news of this, he gave orders that
all subjects of those kingdoms who resided in his territory should be taken prisoner and sentenced to death
if his uncle was not released. The threat worked and
his uncle was sent home.

Both Cacella and Cabral reckoned that they were little more than
a month's journey from the Jesuits who had established a centre at
Tsaparang. Occasionally they obtained news of them, not from the
priests themselves, for they were still unaware of Cacella's presence, but from lamas coming from there. This was not surprising,
for there were frequent contacts between Bhutan and western Tibet
thanks to the prestige enjoyed in both countries by the Red Hat
lamas. Cacella had sent three letters by means of the lamas to
Tsaparang to be sent on from there to Goa, but had received none
in return. In writing to Goa he says little about the character of the
people of Bhutan among whom he has been living, but gives the
first description of their appearance to reach Europe. 'Their skin,'
he writes,

> is fair, though it hardly seems so because of their lack
> of personal cleanliness. All wear their hair long so that
> it covers their ears and part of their forehead. There is
> no hair as a rule on their face, but they carry on their
> chest small, well-made tongs which they use just for
> the purpose of pulling out hairs. Their arms are bare
> and the body is covered from neck to knee with a
> woollen garment, while another large piece of cloth
> serves as a cloak. They gird themselves with a leather
> belt studded with neatly worked small plates; their
> bracelets and amulets, which are generally worn, are
> also cleverly made and engraved. As a rule they go
> barefoot, though they know the use of leather boots
> and woollen stockings, especially when they go on
> their travels. Their weapons consist of bows and
> arrows, short swords and daggers of excellent iron
> that are skilfully adorned.

Following in the footsteps of the priests in the early part of the nineteenth century, Samuel Turner makes similar observations on the
people of Paro, remarking that they were famous for forging arms,

especially swords and daggers, and for making barbs for their arrows.

In spite of the compromise suggested by Cacella that he should continue his journey to the north and west while Cabral remained behind, it was clear that the rajah would not consent graciously to his departure. Come what might, Cacella was now determined to escape their forced detention. Making friends with a lama who was ill-disposed to the rajah, he obtained from him everything he required for the journey to Utsang, including an escort. Within twenty days he reached Shigatse, the residence of the King of Utsang. He was the first European to enter central Tibet.

Lying at the centre of a small, heavily populated plain near the Tangpo River, Shigatse was the second city of Tibet, an important junction on the caravan route from Lhasa to Nepal and the road to western Tibet, Kashmir and Sinkiang. It was also the traditional seat of the Panchen Lama, who ruled four thousand monks in the monastery of Tashi-Lhumpo to the west of the town. When earlier the Dalai Lama was recognized in Lhasa as the political leader of Tibet, the spiritual supremacy of the country seems to have become invested in the abbot of Tashi, the Panchen Lama, the descendant of the Buddha of Light. His succession, like that of the Dalai Lama, resulted from a direct reincarnation; on his death his spirit was also said to pass into the body of a recently born child, whose identity was established by a series of exacting tests. For generations after the visit of the Fathers to Shigatse, the Chinese, when it suited their purpose, would back the Panchen Lama in rivalry to the Dalai Lama in the Potala. Receiving a kind reception at his castle from the King at Shigatse, Cacella at once sent a messenger to the rajah with letters from the ruler of Shigatse, asking that Cabral be allowed to join him. The rajah agreed reluctantly that he could go. Travelling by Pro and Gyantse, Cabral reached Shigatse on 20 January 1628.

At Shigatse the King allowed the two priests to preach to his people. He offered them a residence of their own and provided them with ample provisions. He then appointed a servant to keep him informed of anything further they might need. As elsewhere, the King was to keep the strangers at his court.

The king at the time was Deba Camba, a young man of twenty-two, of fair complexion and in good health. 'The royal town [Shigatse],' Cabral was to write later, lies at the foot of a mountain on the summit of which stands a fortress, the residence of the King and all his attendants, along with his guard of soldiers. The fort is constructed on the Portuguese plan and lacks only artillery. The houses within the enclosure are gilded and painted inside, especially in the wing containing the King's apartments, which indeed are worth seeing. There are some rooms full of trinkets of every sort, for he is a rich man and has things from everywhere. There are hangings in all the rooms: the plainer ones are Chinese damask, but there are others finer than any to be seen in Portugal. His retainers dress very neatly but, on the other hand, the people wear much the same clothes as in other kingdoms.

Utsang, Cabral believed, was a large and densely populated kingdom. The villages were numerous and the climate was cold. 'In January and February,' Cabral continues, 'I have crossed several frozen streams on horseback, but the snowfall is insignificant. There are large cornfields and I have seen no country more like Alemtejo in Portugal than this.'

With a comparatively mild climate and with a friendly ruler, Shigatse had much going for it as a centre for a mission. The great lamas in the country lived each in his own town. Here in Shigatse the monastery was situated 'two cannon-shots' from the fortress on a prominent ridge of the same rock about half a mile to the east of the town on the left bank of the river. It was an important religious centre, with thousands of monks housed in innumerable buildings on the terraced slopes below the fortress.

The two priests were also entertained by the lamas of the Tashi-Lhumpo, the great Tibetan monastic college. Here Cacella was convinced that he had found 'the gateway to Tartary, to China, and to many other countries besides', for this was not only the religious but also the geographical centre of Lamaism. From here it was possible to reach Tsaparang and the mission there in four weeks by travelling westward down the well-worn trail along the valley of the river Tsangpo. It was the route regularly taken by a constant stream of traders from northern to eastern Tibet and by pilgrims visiting the tomb of Tsong-Kapa, the founder of the Yellow sect.

When in Bhutan Cacella believed he had seen in the religious rites and regular prayers of the people vestiges of a lost Christianity. But his companion Cabral came to think very differently. 'I begin to believe that these countries are pagan,' he reflected, 'both because they say they are, and because I have found that they have the same pagodas as in the kingdom of Nepal and some kingdoms of Bengal. They differ from the latter only in not having their superstitions in regard to caste and food.' Nevertheless, towards the end of his long letter, he returned to the fabled land of Cathay, indicating once more how little Ricci's letters and Goes's protestations had availed in dislodging the ancient belief in the existence of this country. 'As regards Cathayo,' he writes,

> the more we learn of that country, the less we know of it. One of the King's lamas told me that there was a country called Cata, whose religion he did not know for certain, but of which he had been told that it was very old and that it differed from that of these countries. The road to it, he said, is by Coscar [Kashger], a well-known town: this accords with the report of Father Jerónimo Xavier, in which the same town is mentioned.

At the end of January Cabral, leaving Cacella behind, set out to report back to India on the prospects of a mission in Shigatse. His object was also to discover by way of Nepal a safer and easier route from Shigatse to India than the way they had taken through Bhutan. No details exist of his winter journey under deep snow through the Himalayan passes at an altitude of many thousand feet. With his guides carrying letters to the King of Nepal, he passed through Kuti to Katmandu, his capital, and from there along the trail to Patna. Thirty years later two other Jesuits, Johannes Grueber and Albert d'Orville, were to follow this same route. Among Europeans Cabral was the first European to mention the name Tibet and the first to enter the country. Writing on 17 June 1628, after his return to India, Cabral is eloquent on the prospects of a mission in Shigatse: 'I have come,' he says,

> to settle some business in connection with this mission [Shigatse], which I think may become one of the most glorious of the Society of Jesus; it is the gateway to the whole of Tartary, China, and many other pagan countries. . . . The road to those countries is not through

Estevão Cacella and João Cabral

Cocho but through Nepal, which borders on Mogor. In Patana [Patna] and Raiamol [Raimahal] the road is perfectly safe and used by many traders. The King [of Shigatse] gave me a captain to conduct me to Nepal. ...About the kingdom of Nepal I shall write to you at greater length later when I get news from Father Cacella.

It is difficult to determine why six months after Cabral had left for India via Nepal, his companion Cacella, after promising the King to return, took the same road to Bengal by which the two Fathers had come. It is likely, however, that his health was failing; or he may have wanted to plead with his Superiors in India for more priests in order to establish a permanent mission at Shigatse. Whatever his motives, it is known that Cacella had first set out for the mission at Tsaparang, but had to return to Shigatse defeated by the weather.

Cacella arrived in Bengal in poor health in June 1629, but was heartened to hear that a priest, Fr Manuel Diaz, a comparatively young man of thirty-seven who had been working for fifteen years in Cochin, had already been appointed to Shigatse. On learning that Cabral was in Cocho with Diaz, Cacella went at once to join them. In September, after resting for three short months, Cacella, in fulfillment of his promise to the rajah, set out once more for Shigatse, taking Diaz with him, but leaving Cabral behind on business connected with the projected mission. He intended to send for him the following January.

The crossing of the Himalayas proved too much for Diaz's health. He died on 3 November in a village called Oacho in the kingdom of Morog. Cacella continued alone to Shigatse, where he arrived on 30 April 30. He was so wretchedly ill that he died six days later at the age of forty-five. The King was so impressed by the manner of his death that he sent at once for Cabral. But it was winter when Cabral received the call and he could do nothing. The following year the King repeated his summons, dispatching an escort of soldiers to bring him back. Cabral obeyed and was again kindly received at Shigatse. But while he was there, events in Tibet decided the fate of the mission, which had claimed two out of the three priests assigned to it. A fierce power struggle erupted between the lamas of the Yellow sect and the rajahs of the old

79

regime. With help from Mongolia, Nyavang Lobsang became all-powerful in eastern Tibet. He had been head of the Tashi-Lhumpo Monastery and had advanced in his career with the help of the Tartar prince Gushi Kahn. Nyavang is said to have begun construction of the Potala at Lhasa and visited Peking; according to some accounts, he received from the Emperor temporal and spiritual authority over the whole of Tibet. Declaring himself the first Dalai Lama, he established the dynasty of Dalai Lamas and made the Yellow sect, the Gelupe, paramount in Tibet.

In May or June 1632 Cabral returned to Hugli. By winning the favour of the King, he had incurred the suspicion and enmity of the lamas. It was the end of the mission that had held such great expectations of success and had already been designated the Cathay Mission. All that has remained of it was Fr Cacella's grave in Shigatse.

A report from Tsaparang dated 30 August 1635 regarding the prospects of the mission there and the one begun by Fr Cacella concluded that the risks were so great and the promise of success so uncertain that both should be abandoned. The report was acted upon.

Ten years later a voice was raised in protest. Fr Simon de Figueiredo, who in 1626 had accompanied Cacella to Dacca, wrote to Rome: 'Want of men and money have compelled us to give up the mission, but we cannot leave the country entirely to itself. Great sacrifices have been made for it. Brother Goes has died in discovering it; and after him Cacella and Diaz. . . . Let us not be less generous. The people are worth it. . . . conditions there are more favourable than in Japan or Ethiopia.'

Tibet, however, was only an episode in Cabral's long career. At different times he was involved in work in Cochin (India), in Japan, in Tonkin, then at Malacca and Macao. He died in Goa on 4 July 1669.

[1]'The Voyage of Master Ralph Fitch ... Begun in the Year 1853' in C. Wessells, *Early Jesuit Travellers in Central Tibet* (The Hague, 1924).
[2]Ibid., 134.

[3]Samuel Turner, *An Account of the Embassy to the Court of Teshoo Lama in Tibet* (London, 1806), 180.
[4]L.A. Waddell, *The Buddhism of Tibet* (1895), 242.
[5]R.C. Markham, *Narrative of the Mission of George Bogle to Tibet* (London, 1879), 214.

Johannes Grueber
and Albert d'Orville

Today a journey from Peking to Koko-Nor and from there to Lhasa and through Nepal to Agra would be regarded as a remarkable feat. About two hundred and sixty or seventy years ago, however, this same journey was undertaken by two Jesuit priests, Johannes Grueber, an Austrian, and Albert d'Orville, a Belgian, whose achievement remains largely unknown and unsung. Its details are scanty and there exists no complete account of the expedition. The story nevertheless can be pieced together from various sources; the most important of these are five letters written by Grueber to correspondents in Europe and India, his answers to questions put to him by the archduke of Tuscany, the eulogy of d'Orville, who died at Agra on his return to India, and, lastly, an important account of their travels supplied by Grueber to Fr Athanasius Kircher on his return to Rome.

Athanasius Kircher, who was born in Fulda in 1601, already had a reputation as a scientist before he began teaching mathematics at the Roman College, the international seminary founded by Ignatius of Loyola. There was hardly a department of science or geography that did not interest him. He made a study of magnetism, demonstrating the fascination chalk lines exerted on hens, and in so doing initiated an inquiry into hypnotic phenomena; he invented the magic lantern, and his name is connected with the speaking trumpet and the invention of a common alphabet for the deaf and dumb. He also drew up the first cartographic representation of ocean currents and, in order to make scientific observations on the cause of earthquakes, had himself lowered into the crater of Vesuvius. He published his investigations in his *Mundus Subterraneus*, a twelve-volume study of earthquakes, volcanoes, underground animals, rivers and plants.

As a young priest Kircher had hoped to follow Matteo Ricci to Peking. On his return to Europe after crossing from Peking to Smyrna, Grueber had several meetings with Kircher, who illustrated his *China Illustrata* with sketches made by Grueber on his epic journey. After Grueber had left Rome for his native Austria, before completing his report, Kircher solicited further information from him. Replying to his request from Gorz in Austria on 26 February 1666, Grueber informed Kircher that he would shortly be sending him the whole journal with the complete history of the kingdom of Barantola (Lhasa), which Kircher would be free to dispose of as he wished; he would try to send him some more drawings of remarkable things he had seen on his journey.

However, Kircher was forced to go to press in 1667 before he had heard further from Grueber, but he still hoped to add details when his book went into a second edition. Grueber criticized the first edition and promised to send a list of points that required correction. He gave as an example Kircher's representation of the Emperor of China carrying a stick and accompanied by a dog, as it appeared in *China Illustrata*. This, says Grueber, will be taken as an insult in that country: the Emperor should be represented either standing or sitting at a table covered with books and mathematical instruments. Accordingly he requests Kircher to correct this in the Italian edition he was preparing, an edition that seems never to have been published. Grueber then adds that he himself would state this clearly in his own journal, which he was working on and hoped to publish in 1671. Ever since his return to Austria, he complains, he has been unable to find time to work on it. He appears to have been serving as a military chaplain at the time he wrote this. Nevertheless, on 2 May 1671 he wrote again to Kircher: 'Being engaged in continuous very hard work among the soldiers, I have been unable to finish the work I have begun, but now that I have some more leisure I hope with God's help to have the whole completed before the autumn.' Grueber's last letter to Kircher is dated 13 January 1670; he wonders whether his very dear friend is buried in the subterranean world or has been swept away in ecstasy to the regions above, because he has not answered one little word 'to all his letters'. It is not known whether the journal was ever completed. One thing would seem certain: with all his gifts of acute observation, Grueber found it easier to talk than to write about his almost incredible achievements.

Johannes Grueber was born at Linz on the Danube on 28 October 1623, and entered the Society at the age of eighteen. It was only while he was studying theology that a fellow Austrian, Fr Bernard

Diestel, recently returned from the Near East, suggested to him that he might offer himself for the Chinese Mission. Accordingly, in 1656 Grueber set out for Rome, where he and Diestel were instructed by the Jesuit General, Fr Goswin Nickel, not to take the usual sea route from Lisbon to Goa, but to strike overland from Asia Minor and Persia through central Asia to China; the aim was to find a new route to the East that was less costly in lives than the voyage round the Cape, where freebooters, seasickness, the doldrums and storms always took a heavy toll on missionaries before they could reach their destination. In fact, Diestel himself had only recently been released after a period of captivity at the hands of corsairs. The loss of lives, already heavy, continued to mount in the course of the next twenty years: of the twelve Jesuits, for instance, who sailed in March 1573 from Lisbon to the mission in China, only one arrived in Macao. Two among the dead were able mathematicians who, right up to the time of their death, had kept a detailed account of the voyage: they recorded the stifling heat on a becalmed sea off the coast of Africa, the putrid water they had to drink, the sight of sick men dying in agonized convulsions. And in that same year seven Jesuits destined for the Portuguese mission in Angola died when their galleon was lost at sea. By the year 1684 it was reckoned that in the hundred years since Ricci arrived in China, only a hundred priests had reached Macao of the six hundred that had sailed for the mission.

It may also have been the intention of the Jesuit General, Fr Goswin Nickel, to free himself from Portugal's restriction that all missionaries of whatever nationality travelling to her colonies must sail in Portuguese ships. The General's directives for the two priests were simply outlined. They were to go first to Isfahan, win the Shah's favour, and offer him presents. They should stay there until they had learned Persian and Arabic. While there they were to gather all the information they could about trade between Persia and China. If relations between the two countries permitted, they were to join a caravan to China. The more northern route was recommended as being the shortest. The instructions insisted on detailed inquiries over a wide field: the latitude of the more important towns; the conditions of the roads; particulars regarding the local manners, customs, government, language and religion; the departures of caravans, their itineraries and stopping places, and

Johannes Grueber and Albert d'Orville

the possibility of sending letters by them. Since Samarkand was only some seventy or eighty miles from Su-cheu and the Great Wall, it was most important that the stretch between the two places be exhaustively surveyed. Should there be a chance of establishing a mission station in Samarkand or elsewhere, they were to apply to the French Jesuits in Isfahan for help. But they were to remember that their main purpose was to open up an overland route to China and discover how postal communications could be established with Peking. This was particularly urgent, because in 1660 letters written by Jesuits in China took five years to reach Rome.

The briefing was clear, but the knowledge of central Asia on which it was based was, of course, both misleading and contradictory.

Sailing to Smyrna, the two priests set out from there overland and reached Isfahan shortly before Christmas 1656. Here they found the so-called 'northern route' closed to them: the shah was arming in preparation for war against the prince of Samarkand. There was no alternative but to set out for Goa. Making their way to Bander Àbbas, they crossed to Ormuz, where they took a ship to Surat in the Gulf of Cambay.

At Surat they were informed that the Dutch were blockading Goa. After waiting ten months to continue their journey, they and four other Jesuits were taken on board by an English captain and given a free passage to Macao, reaching there at the end of July 1658.

Grueber stayed a very short time in Macao before he was assigned to Peking to assist the famed Adam Schall, the German Jesuit from Cologne, in the Peking observatory, which had been entrusted to the Jesuits by the first Manchu emperor. In 1644 the great Ming dynasty that had ruled China since 1363 had fallen as the Manchu had poured through the eastern end of the Chinese Wall. Schall, seen in his letters as a man with a robust and hearty sense of humour, was no less remarkable, in a different area of science, than Athanasius Kircher. He had been in China for thirty-six years. Now a master of flawless Chinese, he had worked on the reform of the Chinese calendar, had constructed astronomical instruments, had written a hundred and thirty-seven treatises in Chinese and had gained widespread prestige by predicting solar and lunar eclipses; he had also manufactured cannons for the last

Ming emperor, drawn up plans for the fortification of Peking, built a baroque church, studied mining methods and designed a sailing boat for the Emperor.

In China Schall was reckoned the equal of their own famous astronomers of legendary times. He was among the closest friends and confidants of the Emperor, who frequently summoned him to the palace at night for scientific discussions. When he was kept there until late at night, he was given an escort of two Manchu princes to see him safely home to the Jesuit residence. At the time of Grueber's arrival he had become the president of the Mathematical Tribunal and mandarin of the first class. In Peking there is a portrait of him as an old man, said to have been painted by Grueber himself.

During his ten months waiting for a ship in Surat, Grueber had already shown his competence in science. With the instruments he carried to mark every place on the 'northern route' to China, he had fixed the latitude of the town and calculated its longitude at the time of the lunar eclipse in December 1657. It was to be expected, therefore, that on his arrival in Peking he would be assigned to assist Fr Schall, who at that time was drawing up plans for a new observatory.

It was also a time of crisis for the Chinese Mission. The approach to Macao by sea was almost closed. The Dutch were gradually eroding the power of the Portuguese in the Far East. The governor general of Batavia, Jan Maetsuiker, had at this time two notorious lieutenants, Bort and Spelman, who incessantly harassed the Portuguese, holding up every vessel sailing in or out of Macao. Shortly before Grueber's arrival the Dutch had seized two ships carrying funds destined for the Chinese Mission. The Jesuit treasurer, left without resources, borrowed twelve thousand scudi and wrote in desperation to Rome, proposing that an appeal should be made to the European princes for a subsidy.

In this critical situation it became more urgent than ever to find an overland supply route to the mission. The Fathers, however, were now in no position to finance an expedition. An appeal was made to Schall: he was asked to call upon the Emperor to obtain from him the required funds. The Emperor was now old and in frail health; should he die there was no certainty that his successor would continue to show the same favour to Schall. Other pressures were mounting. Many of the Fathers were, in Grueber's words, 'verging on old age'. The number of Christians was growing fast and there appeared little hope of replacements coming by sea. And there were other matters pressing for a solution from Rome, such as the compatibility of ancestor worship with Christian practice; these required a priest personally to explain the complexity of the problem. Letters were inadequate and there was no certainty that they would arrive.

Already before Matteo Ricci's death in 1610, some had objected to his regarding certain so-called 'Chinese Rites' as compatible with Christian practice. The three main usages in question were the forms of veneration rendered by the Chinese to their dead, certain ceremonies in honour of Confucius, and the use of the existing Chinese terms for God and the Supreme Being. 'I have opened the door for you,' were Ricci's last words to his fellow Jesuits. A few years later the door was opened still further when the Jesuits were granted permission by the Pope, Paul IV, to use Chinese in the celebration of Mass and the sacraments, and, for the benefit of newly ordained Chinese priests, in the breviary also.

When Adam Schall reached Peking, the controversy threatened to undermine the achievement of Ricci and his successors at the imperial court. The attack focused mainly on Schall himself. As a mandarin of the first class, he conformed to the custom of his peers, bending his knee to the Emperor on ceremonial state occasions, thus laying himself open to accusation of superstitious practices and, still worse, of emperor worship. Charges against him in particular had already been lodged in Rome; but since the very existence of the now flourishing Church in China depended on the goodwill and prestige he had won with the Emperor, it was crucial for the survival of the mission that the Jesuit case should be presented to the Pope.

Grueber's attempt to find a safe and if possible shorter overland route to Rome now became still more urgent. Among the papers he and d'Orville carried with them were three long, tightly packed letters, now in the Jesuit archives, the first by Schall himself; the second by Ferdinand Verbiest, a Belgian priest, later Schall's eminent successor in the observatory; and the last by Grueber himself, who in his comparatively brief stay in Peking had formed a close friendship with Schall. No greater motivation could have been given the two travellers setting out on their hazardous enterprise.

Schall, who many years earlier had foreseen the critical state of the mission, had himself studied the trade routes in central Asia, calling on the caravan leaders as they arrived in Peking. His long report listed, among numerous others, routes through northwest India and eastern Bengal. He now succeeded in obtaining the support of the Emperor, who granted the necessary permission for them to leave the country and supplied them abundantly with jewels, money and equipment – everything that was required for the journey.

After two years in Peking, Grueber, who had been commissioned in Rome to pioneer an overland route from Europe to Peking, was now chosen by the overall Superior of the Far East Mission, Simão da Cunha, to continue his exploration in reverse. The route taken by Goes was rejected as too long and impracticable; the way through China, Tonkin, Siam and Pegu was also discarded: it involved too many peoples, languages, and customs, as Grueber himself pointed out. Da Cunha favoured the northerly route via Samarkand, reckoning that it would take no more than eight or nine months: he calculated that it was only eighty leagues from Su-cheu to Samarkand. Grueber was to gather all the information he could possibly get about caravan routes, note down the times of their departure and arrival and the places they visited; he was to determine whether they were a safe method of dispatching letters and, finally, whether a mission station could be established at Samarkand that could be served from the Chinese Mission. Since money for the mission would be dispatched overland, the purpose of their journey was to be kept secret. The route through Tibet that was finally taken was not considered even as an alternative. It lay through unknown territory, unmapped and, as Grueber rightly claimed, untravelled until then by any European. Aware of the experiences of Goes, Grueber was anxious to have a companion. Accordingly, his superior in Peking accepted the offer of Fr Albert d'Orville to accompany him.

D'Orville was the son of Louis, comte d'Orville. Born in Brussels on 12 August 1621, he was two years older than Grueber and had lived at the court of the duke of Neuberg before entering the Society in October or November 1646 at Landsberg in Lorraine.

While studying in Louvain he met Fr Martino Martini, the geog-
rapher who won fame by drawing a new map of China for the
Emperor and who at that time was on business for the mission in
Europe. His lecture to the students in the university made such an
impression on d'Orville that he at once volunteered to work in
China and left straight away to finish his studies in Rome.

Leaving Lisbon in 1656 with Martini and seventeen others, they
reached Goa early the following year; but two had died on the
voyage, one had gone mad and a fourth was close to death on his
arrival.

After a year in Goa they set out for Macao on 30 January 1658,
sailing via Macassar (Ujung Pandang) in Indonesia, but some of
the priests were so ill that they had to be left behind. After six
months at sea, they reached Macao on 17 July 1658.

D'Orville was at work in the province of Shan-si when Grueber
asked to have him as his companion. In the course of two years on
the mainland, he had already gained considerable mastery of the
language, which he had been studying with the help of Fr Martini
since he had left Europe. To prepare himself for the journey, he was
posted to the Peking observatory to be trained under Fr Schall in
the kind of geographical determination that would be useful on his
journey. Schall was then in his early seventies and was occupied
mainly in building the new imperial observatory; he died in Peking
in 1666, five years after Grueber and d'Orville set out on their
return voyage to Europe.

Nothing is known of the mapping equipment the two priests
took with them on their expedition, but thanks to Schall's influence
with the Emperor, they were given an imperial passport, letters of
recommendation to the local authorities in the northwest provinces, and a large sum of money; they also carried letters and reports
on the state of the mission. Moreover, Grueber also took his sketch-
ing equipment.

Sven Hedin rightly states that Grueber's account of his journey
is not as impressive as the journey itself. 'He had, it is true, a bird's
sense of the lie of the land, but he lacked the bird's blithe tongue.
His notes are as dry as the rocks of Tibet.' He has little to say about
the landscape and is silent on the progress of the little caravan.
His jottings are mainly figures, topographical notes and a daily
record of distances covered. Accompanying them, however, are

very accurate and detailed sketches that embellish his dry account of his astonishing achievement in travelling the entire distance from Peking to Smyrna through central districts of Asia hitherto unknown in the West.

The expedition got under way on 13 April 1661. Taking the well-travelled route through Taj-Juan and Sianfu, the eastern end of the Silk Road, they arrived at Lanchow, the capital of the province of Kansu. From here there was regular commerce with Sinkiang in the extreme northwest of China. Instead of taking the Silk Road from here, they decided instead to travel to Hsining (Si-ning), the capital of Tsinghai Province, which for centuries had traded with Tibet in wool, hides, salt and timber.

The travellers purposely chose to go this way, but it is difficult to explain their reasons. Fr Schall must have outlined for them the route of the Silk Road. He had been in Singanfu in 1630 and had made a study of the organization of China's trade routes with Central Asia. While there he had persuaded the great silk magnate Mirjudin to give him twenty interviews, during which the merchant had described each stage of the hundred and nineteen days' journey along the caravan route from the Chinese frontier town of Su-cheu, where Bento de Goes had died, to Bukhara. Other merchants told him about the continuation of the trade route to Merv, Meshed, Tabris and on to Aleppo in Syria. On the basis of this information, Schall had calculated that he could cover the distance from the Mediterranean to the Great Wall in two hundred and fifty-five days.

Schall had sent the result of his researches to Rome, where no doubt Grueber saw them before sailing to Smyrna. There can hardly be any doubt that in the months of preparation for the journey the two priests had discussed this well-established route. Possibly on his arrival at Lanchow Grueber had received news of fighting in the area that made it hazardous to take the Silk Road, especially in view of the important papers he was carrying to Rome. Or did he recall the fate of Bento de Goes, who had once travelled along the middle stretch of the Silk Road in the opposite direction and before his death in Su-cheu had cautioned Ricci of its terrible dangers? Whatever his reasons, Grueber turned towards Tibet, taking a route that Schall only briefly mentioned in his report to Rome.

1. *Bento de Goes*

2. *Matteo Ricci (left)*

3. *Lhasa and the Potala*

4. Tibetan hermit (nineteenth century)

5. Adam Schall

6. *Kalmak Tartars*

7. Travel in the Himalayas I (nineteenth century)

8. Travel in the Himalayas II (nineteenth century)

Continuing their journey, the two priests reached Hsining (Si-ning) at the end of June after more than four weeks on the road. Here they stayed for a month making preparations for the next stage of their journey. Grueber used this halt to determine the latitude of the town. He describes it as a large, populous place of considerable importance because of its closeness to the Great Wall, which at that point was wide enough for six horsemen to ride abreast. He adds that this was the first Gate on the Wall, where traders had to wait for permission to enter the Middle Kingdom: from there to Su-cheu, he was told, was eighteen days' travel.

Today no part of the Great Wall is to be seen at Hsining. But a Jesuit priest visiting the town in 1720 explains Grueber's statement. 'At its western extremity it is just a mud wall or in many places a terrace gone to ruin.' It is true that here and there he found towers of stone brickwork, but most of them were built of mud. Grueber explains that at a distance of three miles from the town walls stood such a fort with an armament of three rows of guns. Through here foreigners had necessarily to pass before entering a suburb of the town that was reserved for Muslims, just as was the case at Su-cheu, eighteen days' journey from Si-ning. The destruction of the wall here only sixty years after Grueber's visit resulted from the Dzungarians' repeated rebellions against the Chinese; such an uprising may in fact have been the reason for Grueber's choice of the route via Tibet.

After two weeks in Si-ning, Grueber and d'Orville left the Chinese Wall on 13 July 1661 and struck west into Tartary, a country unknown to Europeans. It took them only three days to reach Koko-Nor, meaning in Tartian language 'the Blue Sea'. The sea has no outlet to the ocean, though Grueber and others after him believed it to be the source of the great Yellow River cutting through the length of China; the priests had had to cross and recross this river a number of times on their road to Lanchow. Although the Blue Sea is the largest lake in central Asia, Grueber gives no description of it. The explorer Prejevalsky, who was there in 1872, writes that 'its shores are flat and shelving, its waters salt and undrinkable, but this salt imparts an exquisite dark-blue color to the surface, which excites even the admiration of the Mongols, who have compared it not inaptly to blue silk.'[1]

The next European after Grueber to take this road to Lhasa was the French priest Abbé Régis-Evariste Huc. Setting out in August 1844 from the Mongolian town of Kum-Bum, a short distance across the Chinese border immediately north of Peking, Huc and his companion, Abbé Gabet, travelled through the winter and reached Lhasa in January 1846. Huc's narrative gives a vivid description of every stage of the journey from Koko-Nor to the capital, about which Grueber is silent for the most part, perhaps because his principal concern was for the safety of the letters he was carrying.[2]

Huc speaks of the salt and bitter waters of Koko-Nor that ebb and flow like an ocean and exhale a marine odour that is noticeable at a great distance far into the desert. Though altogether without trees, the vast plain surrounding the lake was crossed by numerous streams that made it excellent pasture for large herds. But the Mongol tribes that set up their tents there were constantly harassed by brigands. Always on the alert against them every hour of the day and night, they tended their cattle on horseback, lance in hand, fusil in sling, and sabre in belt. In his report to Rome, Grueber mentions brigands as one of the dangers of the overland route to China but goes into no detail. Their haunt lay in the deep gorges of the mountain which no one could penetrate without a guide. 'It is said,' writes Huc, 'that these brigands are in the revolting habit of eating the hearts of their prisoners in order to fortify their own courage; but, for that matter, there is no monstrous habit that the Mongols of the Koko-Nor do not unhesitatingly attribute to them.'

Beyond these fertile plains they crossed into what Grueber describes as a 'desertlike territory, partly mountainous, sandy, and exceedingly barren, except for a few strips intersected by small rivers.' It was a region that had been given different names through the centuries. Marco Polo called it Lop, the Tartars Samo, the Chinese Kalmuk, others Caracathai or Black Cathay. 'Animals are not found there,' says Grueber, 'except for a species of big bulls,' no doubt meaning roaming yaks. Huc speaks of the savage and sad nature of the area, arid and stony and producing only a few dry, saltpetrous bushes.

The morose and melancholy tinge of these dismal regions seems to have had its influence on the character of its inhabitants. . . . They say very little, and their language is so rude and guttural that other Mongols can scarcely understand them. Mineral salt and borax abound. You dig holes two or three feet deep and the salt collects therein and crystallizes and purifies of itself. The borax is collected from small reservoirs, which were full to the brim. The Tibetans carry quantities of this into their own country, where they sell it to the goldsmiths and silversmiths, who apply it to facilitate the fusion of metals.

In answer to questions from the archduke of Tuscany, Grueber said that the land was so desolate that no fields were to be seen along the road during the time of their three-month journey to the kingdom of Barantola (Lhasa). Hedin, who made this journey in reverse, states clearly that Grueber must have crossed the Koko-Nor Range and come down on the other side into these salty marshes before climbing the Burkham Mountains, where the pass reaches a height of 4,900 metres. To prepare themselves for the steep and rugged climb, travellers ate two or three cloves of garlic. Horses would refuse to carry their riders; having to go on foot, the men, who were already suffering from mountain sickness, stumbled, fell and rose again; horses were whipped to keep them going; in places 'pestilential vapours' rose from the ground.

But the passage of the Burkham Range was only an apprenticeship for the Shuga Mountains, which they had to cross to reach the high Tibetan Plateau: here at four thousand metres the plateau was broken by numerous cross-ridges and strewn with the bodies and bones of pack animals marking the track for adventurous travellers.

This was perhaps the most testing stretch of their journey. Huc explains that the ascent of Mount Shuga from the north was not difficult, but the descent was arduous in the extreme. Again Grueber mentions snow and ice among the hardships of the overland journey, but it is Huc who fills in the details. 'The opposite side of the mountain,' Huc writes,

> we found so encumbered with snow that the animals were up to their girths in it: they could only advance by a series of convulsive efforts, which threw several of them into gulfs from which it was impossible to extricate them and in which they accordingly perished. We marched in the very teeth of a wind so

strong and so icy that it absolutely at times choked our respiration and despite our thick furs made us tremble lest we should be killed with the cold. In order to avoid the whirlwinds of snow that the wind perpetually dashed in our faces, we adopted the example of some of our fellow travellers who bestrode their horses' backs with their faces to the tail, leaving the animals to follow the guidance of their instinct. When we reached the foot of the mountain and could use our eyes, we found that more than one face had been frozen in the descent.

The only sustenance of travellers even two hundred years later was *tsamba*, made from barley dough. Then every morning before setting out, Huc records, they took a meal and did not eat again until they made camp in the evening. 'As tsamba is not a very toothsome affair,' he writes, 'we could not get down at a time what was required for our nourishment during the day; so we used to make three or four balls of it, with our tea, and keep these in reserve to be eaten from time to time on our road. The hot paste was wrapped in hot linen and then deposited against our breasts. Over it went all our clothes, to wit, a thick robe of sheepskin, then a lamb-skin jacket, then a short fox-skin cloak, and then a great wool overall.' Even under all this clothing, when the tsamba cakes were taken out, they were like balls of ice that the travellers had to eat, at the risk of breaking their teeth, in order to sustain their strength.

Here on the high Tibetan Plateau, as Grueber points out, they were in constant fear of attack by marauders and had to keep a perpetual watch against them. Huc calls this Tibetan wilderness without doubt the most terrible place imaginable. As the ground rose steadily, vegetation became more scarce and the cold became alarmingly intense. . . . From then on death hovered over the poor caravan. Lack of water and pasture quickly exhausted the strength of the animals. Each day pack animals that could no longer drag themselves along had to be abandoned. A little later it was to be the turn of the men. . . . For several days we seemed to be passing through a vast graveyard where exhumed human bones and animal carcasses lay strewn everywhere, telling us that in this land of death and the unleashed forces of nature the caravans that had preceded us had no better fate than we.

Then crossing the Baian-Kara Mountains, they came to the banks of the Mur-Ussa or Blue River. Huc, as he approached the river, saw some dark, shapeless masses ranged across its bed. Drawing nearer he was surprised to find that the curious shapes were nothing other than upwards of fifty wild cattle held fast in the ice. In their attempt to swim across they had become trapped in the ice: their fine heads with their great horns were still above the surface, while the rest of their bodies were fast in the ice, which was so transparent that the whole form of the animals could be seen.

Shortly after crossing the Mur-Ussa they faced the Tangla Mountains. It was in this region that travellers came across the wild ass, reddish in colour and the size of a mule but with a finer body, capable of graceful and lighter movements. 'The head is big and ugly,' wrote Huc, 'contrasting with the elegance of the body. . . . They are so fast that the Tartar and Tibetan horsemen cannot catch up with them. They can only take them by means of an ambush laid at their watering places.' A true species, not a crossbreed, they were impossible to domesticate and use for riding or as pack animals. The region was given over to them along with the chamois, the reindeer and the ibex.

Grueber himself has nothing to say about this part of his journey, but about 1870 Prejevalsky took eight days to cross this harsh range, beating off the fierce attacks of the Tanguts all the time. He writes that

> the ground slowly rises to one of the highest plateaux of Tibet, the southern edge of which, running east to west, is formed by mountains covered with eternal snow. . . . The ascent and descent are very gradual, though the pass followed by the Mongolian caravans lies at an elevation of 4,990 metres.[3]

The Franciscan friar William of Rubruck, crossing this area of northern Tibet in the latter part of the thirteenth century, speaks of its inhabitants as very brave men. Some were 'much deformed', in contrast to the Tanguts to their north, who were 'tall and swarthy'.[4]

On the far side of the Tangla Range Grueber and d'Orville would have changed their beasts of burden at Nag-chu. From there to

Lhasa the road was impracticable for horses and camels, which usually had to be replaced by yaks. Unknown in Europe, these animals appear not to have attracted comment from Grueber; but the Franciscan William of Rubruck, meeting them in northern Tibet among the Tangut in the middle of the thirteenth century, had described them for the information of his brethren in Flanders as 'very strong oxen with tails all hair, like horses, and hairy bellies and backs'. He goes on: 'They are shorter in the leg than other oxen but very much stronger. They draw the large dwellings of the Mongols and they have graceful, long curved horns which are so very sharp that their tips have to be cut off.'[5]

At Nag-chu, where they exchanged their horses for yaks, the caravans took special guard against robbers. 'The inhabitants of this Tibetan village,' wrote Huc,

> are remarkable for their peculations, robbing every Mongol or other caravan that comes to the place, in the most shameful manner. At night they creep into the travellers' tents and carry off whatever they can lay their hands on; and in broad daylight they exercise their deplorable ingenuity with a coolness, a presence of mind, and an ability that might arouse envy in the most distinguished Parisian thieves.

They were now in territory belonging to the Kingdom of Barantola (Tibet). Their next objective was the Monastery of Jang Reting Gompa, eighty kilometres north of Lhasa. It was then only left to them to cross the Trans-Himalayan Range by the Penpo-la Pass at fifty-four hundred metres before they came in sight of Lhasa, 'which the Chinese call Cam, the Tartars Barantola, and foreigners Lass'. As they drew nearer they saw black tents that speckled the landscape, then numerous groups of pilgrims repairing to the city and the endless engraved inscriptions on either side of the road.

They arrived on 8 October 1661, three months after leaving the Great Wall on 13 July. The two priests had no intention of establishing a mission. They adhered strictly to the instructions given them in Macao: they had come in search of an overland route to Europe. On their arrival they were submitted to various questionings and were later summoned to the presence of the King, who received them graciously and gave them a royal diploma to

continue their journey. However, their caravan was dispersed at Lhasa and they had to wait a month or more before they could continue their journey.

D'Orville and Grueber were almost certainly the first Europeans to set foot in Lhasa, though it is often claimed that Oderic de Pordenone was there in the year 1328. 'Oderic of Pordenone,' it has recently been said, 'had never traversed Tibet proper, had never been at Lhasa—a feat with which he has been unduly credited and to which he himself lays no claim. The honour of being the first European to reach Lhasa belongs to the two Jesuit Fathers, Grueber and d'Orville, who spent two months there in 1661.'[6]

It is not known where Grueber and his companion stayed at Lhasa. But he reports briefly on the government of the country at that time. There are, he says, two kings. One, called the Deva (Deba), is of ancient Tartar stock and conducts the government; the other is the Great Lama, who is worshipped as a deity and lives in seclusion in the precincts of the palace. The priests did not visit him in person, because they had scruples about conforming to the ceremonies prescribed before admission to an audience. However, Grueber copied a portrait of the Dalai Lama that was hung up at the entrance to the palace and made sketches of the town and its people which were reproduced in Kircher's *China Illustrata*. He painted various temples with their grotesque statues. He was the first traveller in central Asia to mention the prayer wheel, of which he made a sketch. He made the first comprehensive survey of the city and with extraordinary accuracy fixed Lhasa's position on the map.

The most famous and most frequently reproduced of Grueber's sketches is that of the Potala, which he calls the Bietala. It has a curious covered carriage in the foreground drawn by two horses with four men marching ahead of it, seemingly armed, and a fifth following behind. This is probably a fancy of the engraver, for it has always been said that wheeled vehicles were then unknown among the Tibetans. The Chinese, in fact, had invented or used the wheel centuries earlier. On the other hand, Grueber's sketch may well be correct. Heinrich Harrer, the Austrian mountaineer who had escaped from an internment camp in northern India during the war, while he was working in Lhasa on a construction project for the Dalai Lama, uncovered great blocks of stone that he was convinced could only have been transported to the site by mechanical means. This led Harrer to surmise that in earlier centuries the Tibetans may well have known the wheel but had either abandoned it or forgotten its use.

But Grueber's drawing of the Potala was the only one available until the building was photographed in 1901. When his engraving is compared with the numerous photographs taken by members of Younghusband's expedition, it appears that at the time of Grueber's visit only the main building had been completed and that the two wings were a later addition. Grueber was in Lhasa in 1662; but the building had been started in 1642 when Nyavang Lobsang became ruler of Central Tibet. As we saw in the previous chapter, Nyavang had been head of the Tashi-Lhumpo Monastery and had advanced in his career thanks to the assistance of the Tartar prince Gushi Khan. In recognition of his services, Gushi Khan was made military commander of Lhasa with the title of King but under the suzerainty of Nyavang Lobsang.

In 1652, nine years before Grueber passed through Lhasa, Nyavang Lobsang had visited Peking, where he was acknowledged by the Emperor as the Great (Dalai) Lama. Grueber says that he was the seventh incarnation.

Kircher retails the curious information gathered from Grueber about the revolting medicines, both preventive and curative, that were distributed in the Dalai Lama's name. Desideri and others have confirmed all this. However, a Japanese Buddhist discussing these medicines in 1909 writes, 'To do justice to this superstition I ought to add that the common Tibetans are kept entirely in the dark as to the ingredients of the pills; they are taken as medicines prepared by the Grand Lama himself according to a certain secret formula, and the shocking secret is known only to a select few who are entitled to attend the Dalai Lama's court.'[7]

Towards the end of November Grueber and d'Orville left Lhasa, taking the difficult but well-travelled route to Katmandu. 'After four days we were confronted with high mountains called "Langur": this is a generic term used by the Nepalese for any snow-covered mountain range. Here in the rarified atmosphere of the high passes of the Himalayas, a word not known to the simple people, they found breathing difficult.

After the travellers had passed through Nesti, at the second

milestone, the road became hazardous, as a Capuchin missionary described it some years later:

It climbs and drops by very narrow stairs of loose stones; above are high rocks, below an awesome precipice. The paths in this precipitous area are very narrow and all the time wind along the sides of high mountains. Often unstable rocks are linked by little hanging bridges which have no hand-rail. One has to cross these unsteady, narrow bridges, made of poles and branches, a dozen times. Your fear is increased by the perpendicular depth into which you gaze as you cross, not to mention the mighty roar of the water-rushing through the boulders below. To help travellers, natives have made some footholds in the rocks, which will fit, if not the whole foot, at least the heel.[8]

It was a month after leaving Lhasa that Grueber and his companion arrived at Kuti (Nilam Dzong), which is merely mentioned as a stopping place by Grueber.

Beyond Kuti the two priests faced an even more severe test of their endurance: Grueber records that it took them ten days to reach Katmandu from Kuti; later Desideri took two weeks over this stretch of their journey. In 1871 the Pandit Hari Ram required the same time to complete this terrifying trip. Major T.G. Montgomerie, for whom the pandit was acting, took down his report. He recounted that the hardest section was the first five days between Kuti and Nesti.

Between Nilam and Listi Blansar he [the pandit] followed the general course of the Bhotia Kosi River and though it is but twenty-five miles direct distance between the two places, the explorer had to cross the Bhotia River fifteen times by means of three iron suspension and eleven wooden bridges, each from twenty-four to sixty paces in length. At one place the river ran into a gigantic chasm, the sides of which were so close to one another that a bridge of twenty-four paces was sufficient to span it. This was just below or south of the village of Choksum. Near the bridge the precipices were so impracticable that the path had of necessity to be supported on iron pegs let into the face of the rock, the path being formed by bars of iron and slabs of stone stretching from peg to peg and covered with earth. This extraordinary path is in no place more than eighteen inches and often not more than nine inches in width and is carried for more than one third of a mile (775 paces) along the face of the cliff, at some 1,500 feet above the river, which could be seen roaring below in its narrow bed. The explorer who had seen much difficult ground in the Himalayas, says never in his life had he met anything equal to this bit of path. . . . There are several other smaller pieces of paths between Nilam and Listi Blansar that are nearly so bad but they are fortunately not continuous.[9]

The only European to enter this region before Grueber and d'Orville had been Fr Cabral. In the early part of the twentieth century, the only person permitted to follow him into this secluded area of the Himalayas was the British ambassador to the Court of Katmandu.

When they arrived at Katmandu the two priests found the country in a state of war. The King of Katmandu had joined with his brother Nevagmal, the ruler of Patan, which was about half a day's march from the southeastern point of Katmandu. Led by Nevagmal, the united army took the field against a princeling called Varcam, whose constant raids had been the scourge of the country.

At the start of the campaign Grueber presented Nevagmal with a small spyglass. After spying out the place where Varcam had entrenched himself, Grueber handed the glass to the prince and made him look in the right direction. When he saw the enemy apparently so close, the commander, wholly unaware of the optical illusion, gave orders for his troops to advance and surprised the enemy.

Since the Nepalese chronicles state that the King of Katmandu won a final victory on 19 January 1662, when his forces captured the fortified town of Theni (Timi or Dimi), Grueber and d'Orville would have arrived in Katmandu early in January that year. The present of the spyglass and some mathematical instruments so

captivated the King that he begged the Fathers to stay, and finally allowed them to leave only on condition that they undertook to return.

Questioned about Katmandu by Kircher on his return to Rome, Grueber declared that he had found in the Nepalese capital 'nothing whatever lacking for the sustenance of a good life except one thing, namely faith in Christ'. The people, Grueber is reported to have told Kircher, had one unutterably inhumane custom: they threw out from their homes into trenches in the fields men and women when they were close to death with no hope of recovery; they laid them there exposed to the weather without any show of pity or commiseration. After their death they remained in the fields, the prey of rapacious birds, wolves, dogs and beasts. The perpetrators of this inhumanity were persuaded that the dead had found in the entrails of living creatures a truly glorious monument.

'After leaving Katmandu,' Grueber writes briefly,

> I skirted several terrible mountains and at last after thirty-three days reached the Kingdom of Moranga (Muring). I passed through only part of the kingdom and saw only one settlement, called Hetunda [Hitounda]. Then in ten days I arrived at the kingdom of Mogor, that is to say, India, on the other side of the Ganges; then at a league's distance I saw the town of Hagiapor, which is the first one meets on coming from Moranga. It is not far from Minapor [Dinapur] on the Ganges. . . . The next town one meets is Batane [Patna].

From Dinapur it took the priests twenty-five days to travel via Benares and Cawnpore to Agra, where the Jesuits had a long-established church and college. They arrived in the second half of March 1662. They had left Peking on 13 April 1661. D'Orville was a sick man and immediately took to his bed. As his bodily strength drained away, Grueber stood by his bed. On 8 April d'Orville died midway on his journey between China and Europe. In the evening of the same day, he was buried in the old Catholic cemetery at Agra. In 1710 his remains were transferred to the small chapel nearby, Padri Santos, itself a funeral monument to a rich Armenian merchant. In 1906 a Capuchin friar deciphered the inscription on the chapel floor:

AQUI IAZO PE
ALBERTO DOR
VILLE FALECEO
EM AGRA AOS
6 D'ABRIL
1662
BELGA

D'Orville did not live to give his own account of his epic journey. His eulogy was pronounced by his companion, Grueber, the day after his death. Grueber paid tribute to d'Orville's holy life, to his patience and unfailing cheerfulness in the worst trials of their journey, when he would always be optimistic and burst out in song. During the years he spent in China, he would act as infirmarian, cook and dispenser of medicines whenever the need arose. Even in his last illness he was lighthearted.

Writing of the achievement of d'Orville and Grueber, Sven Hedin rightly regrets that they kept no journal. 'It is a very great pity,' he says,

> that so few details of this journey have remained to
> our time. The two Jesuits seem not to have understood
> the great geographical importance of their achieve-
> ment, and they have not even troubled to keep a
> rough diary. We are only able to follow the great
> features of their journey. In some cases, as for instance,
> when Grueber mentions the rivers south of Koko-Nor,
> we cannot with any degree of certainty identify them.

Like the northern Tibetan plain, Grueber's account is arid; he seems to have lacked any narrative gift. He notes a few, brief, bare facts; there is no description of the majestic Himalayan Ranges, nothing about the daily life at Lhasa. It can be said, however, as Sven Hedin points out, that his journey has left its traces on certain ancient maps. If d'Orville did make notes, Grueber does not mention them.

In Rome Grueber was to protest his devotion to d'Orville, 'his dearest companion'. But he himself was now in a state close to exhaustion. In need of a rest, he remained at Agra while the winter made the roads impassable. Later he insisted that he had made no demands on the finances of the province of Goa: he raised the money required for the last part of his journey by selling sketches he had made of Lhasa and other places he had passed.

But he needed a companion who could safely deliver to Rome the letters and the reports he was carrying should he die on the way, so he requested that Fr Heinrich Roth, a scholarly German from Dillingen, should be allowed to join him. The reasons he gave for his choice were that Roth was the only priest in the province of Goa who had himself crossed through Asia Minor and Persia to India, and that he was an accomplished linguist, able to speak Persian. Roth, in fact, was among the first Europeans to gain a complete mastery of Sanskrit, as can be seen in Kircher's *China Illustrata*, which contains five full-page copper-plate engravings of the alphabet and elements of the language, drawn by Roth himself.

Starting on the overland route that led across the plains of northern India, the two priests reached Lahore. It was their intention to attach themselves to a caravan travelling to Persia via Kandahar, but at Lahore they learned that tribal warfare made it unsafe for any European to pass through Afghanistan. After going down the Indus by boat to Tattah, near the modern port of Karachi, they had to wait until 20 January 1663; finally they found a ship that took them in twenty-one days to the Persian port of Congo, the modern Bandar Kungun, a small port west of Bandar Àbbas in the Persian Gulf.

On reaching Isfahan they discovered that a perfidious Armenian merchant would not honour a bill of exchange made out to him, and so they were delayed another month and a half. Leaving Isfahan on 28 May and travelling through Armenia and Turkey, they reached Smyrna on November 27. Taking ship there to Italy, they arrived in Rome on 20 February 1664.

Grueber's first task was to draw up a detailed report on the route he had taken, marking out a chain of bases between Smyrna, where the Jesuits had a college, and Aleppo, Isfahan, Surat, Agra and Nepal.

At the request of the General, Grueber drew up another report on the comparative hazards of the sea and overland routes to China. 'Certainly,' he admitted, 'the land route has its difficulties, but none that a stout-hearted missionary cannot overcome. True, he had to endure extremes of cold and heat, rain, snow and continual travel, all of which could prove too much even for a strong constitution.'

But on the other hand, as he is quick to point out, he had himself experienced the sea passage as well: the constant seasickness, the storms, salted provisions, nausea and the extremely uncomfortable quarters – conditions that can prove too much for human nature. In places, he admits, the land route is infested with bandits who rob and sometimes kill travellers, but he goes on to observe that the sea is never free of pirates. Moreover, there are the contrary winds, the shoals, the storms, which are worse than the robbers and account for more lives. He grants that the sea route would seem quicker and that travelling to China overland takes almost two years if a month or two is allowed for rest and recuperation at different halts on the way. 'It has also been said,' he concludes, 'that greater expense is involved in travelling overland. But I am not ready to agree with this. I have made inquiries and reckon that the outlay is much the same either way.'

Before his death at Agra, d'Orville had given his own assessment of the overland route to China. In recommending it in preference to the sea passage, he proposed that a station should be established in Si-ning: the city was, so to speak, the main gateway to China, where a great concourse of merchants gathered on business, and there were others resident there. Moreover, the place was free from Muslim domination; money for the mission in China could be directed there in either of two ways. There were Armenian merchants resident in Venice or Leghorn who could be trusted to transmit money to the Fathers in Smyrna or Aleppo; they in turn could send it on to the French Fathers at Isfahan in Persia, who would in turn forward it to Agra through Indian merchants by way either of Surat or Kandahar, and thence through Bengal and Katmandu to China. However, he advised against employing an Armenian who acted also for others in Persia; instead, he recommended seeking out a merchant who used this same means of transmitting his own money or wares.

Along with an account of his journey, Grueber on his return to Rome also presented to the Jesuit General a memorandum on Nepal which carries the same date, 18 March 1664. The friendliness of the Nepalese had made an enduring impression on Grueber, who believed that a rewarding mission could be established among them. He pointed out that in all their years in India the Jesuits had little to show for their work in Agra, Delhi or Srinagar, but much might be expected from a station in Nepal. There were several reasons for this. First and foremost was the docility of the people and their natural bent for religion. There was also the matter of language, which was not all that different from the language spoken in northern India: in fact, any priest leaving the Agra Mission for Nepal would not need to learn a new language. Living expenses there were also far less; and if there was a notable conversion in the country, neighbouring rulers and their people might well accept Christianity. They had none of the Muslims' depraved ways.

There is no evidence, however, that any attempt was made to act on Grueber's memorandum or to establish a mission in Nepal.

While Grueber was absent in Asia there had been strong protests that out of consideration for Royal Patronage the old sea passage should continue to be employed, and that the overland route should be used only in special circumstances. In any case, the three years it had taken Grueber to complete his journey was in itself no recommendation for the route he had pioneered. Because Grueber would certainly not be well received in Lisbon if he embarked from there, he was given special permission to return overland to India and, possibly, China.

Aware of the threats of war between Turkey and Persia, Grueber and Roth were eager to leave immediately. So in April or early May following their arrival in Rome, they set off again. On 10 May Grueber wrote to Kircher from Venice, informing him that war had prevented him from sailing. Therefore he planned another route: he would go to Persia by way of Greater Russia and the Caspian Sea, thus avoiding Turkish territory. When the Jesuits reached Mitau near Riga, they heard that the Tartars of the Lower Volga had formed an alliance with the Poles to check the rising power of the Romanoffs, and that consequently the road to Astrakhan was closed to all travellers from Moscow.

Grueber's health now began to fail. He returned to Austria, where he served for two years as an army chaplain, keeping up a correspondence with Kircher about his astonishing journey. He died at Sarospatak in Hungary on 30 September 1680, at the age of fifty-seven.

[1]N. Prejevalsky, *The Targut Country and Solitudes of Northern Tibet* (London, 1876), vol. 2, 73.
[2]M. Huc, *Travels in Tartary, Tibet and China during the years 1844–46*, trans. W. Hazlitt, vol. 2 (1851), ch. 4. (Because Huc's *Travels* is available in such a large number of editions, both English and French, it is possible only to give a reference to the chapter. The latest English edition was published by the Folio Society in 1982 under the title *Lamas of the Western Heavens*.)
[3]*The Targut Country*, 140.
[4]Christopher Dawson, ed. *The Mission to Asia* (London, 1955), 142.
[5]Ibid.
[6]C. Wessells, *Early Jesuit Travellers in Central Asia, 1603–1721*(The Hague, 1924),189, n.8.
[7]Ibid., 191.
[8]Sven Hedin, *Southern Tibet* (Stockholm, 1917), vol. 3, 6.
[9]T.G. Montgomerie, *Records of the Survey of India*, Part 1, vol. 8, 116.

Ippolito Desideri

In 1716 Ippolito Desideri, an Italian Jesuit, travelled via Kashmir and Ladakh to Lhasa, made an extended stay in the city, received a warm reception from the King and the Dalai Lama, and wrote a long and detailed account of the country. The first European to look on the holy mountain of Meru and the crystal-clear Manasarovar, 'the most beautiful lake in the world', he lived for five years with the monks of a Buddhist monastery. Both Desideri's name and his writings, however, were unknown to the English, Indian, Chinese, and French who in the course of the nine-teenth century attempted and failed, sometimes heroically, to enter the mysterious city that for two centuries had been shrouded from the gaze of foreigners. 'All this I have written,' Desideri stated at the end of his long book, 'after traversing all three Tibets and living in those parts continually for several years and after obtaining a fairly wide and deep knowledge of the language, and after reading and examining with protracted study and serious application a great number of the principal and very abstruse books of the people.'

Desideri's manuscript runs to six hundred and thirty closely written pages without a break until it reaches chapter 13; at that point the writer begins to insert chapter headings. It is a fuller, more authoritative and more wide-ranging description of the country than is found in the spate of books on Tibet written after the military expedition to Lhasa in 1904 led by Sir Francis Younghusband had lifted the veil that had enshrouded the capital for two centuries. Writing in 1935 the Swedish explorer Sven Hedin praises Desideri's contribution to Tibetan studies. 'Add to this,' he writes, 'the general merit of his narrative, the absence of fantastical speculation, the quiet matter-of-fact way in which he gives his observations, and nobody will call it an exaggeration if I regard Ippolito Desideri as one of the most brilliant travellers who ever visited Tibet.' Had Desideri's book been known to the nineteenth-century explorers, there would have been little new in the accounts of their travels.

Desideri's manuscript, now in the Bibliotheca Nazionale in

Florence, was discovered in Pistoia, his native city, in 1876 and edited by Professor Carlo Puini in 1904. As all interest in Tibet at the time was focused on Younghusband's expedition, Desideri's work aroused little notice.

Born in Pistoia on 21 December 1684, Ippolito Desideri came from a well-established family that for several generations had supplied magistrates to the city; in 1504 Domenico Desideri was given the title 'citizen' and granted a coat of arms. One of four sons of Jacopo Desideri and his wife, Madalena, Ippolito was only three when his mother died in 1687. It can be safely assumed that he was educated in the school attached to the Jesuit church in Pistoia. From there he went to Rome, where on 27 April 1700 he entered the Society of Jesus in the novitiate adjacent to the Church of Sant' Andrea on the Quirinal.

As was usual when young men entered the Jesuits, an inventory was made of everything he brought in with him. Desideri had come smartly attired. Among other things, he had two jerkins, a black serge cloak, a pair of fustian trousers, one well-worn black silk shirt and another of fine red silk, four pairs of sleeves, a flint, and two nightcaps.

After his studies at the Roman College, the international seminary staffed by the Jesuits, he was ordained in Rome on 28 August 1712. But before leaving Rome to embark at Lisbon for India, he and his companion, Hildebrand Grassi, were received in audience by the pope, Clement XI, who was keenly interested in missionary work in China, India and the Philippines. Desideri spoke with the Pope about his desire to work in Tibet and was given to understand that the Pope had blessed his proposal to refound the Jesuit mission in Tibet. This first Christian centre had been established at Tsaparang in the province of Hundes in 1626, but had been closed in 1651 after the ruling king was overthrown in a revolution and the Jesuits working there were either imprisoned or expelled.

From time to time other mission areas had been considered. Information continued to be gathered from Armenian traders on new routes into Tibet; volunteers came forward but nothing was done. The losses through sickness had been too great.

On 27 September 1712 Ippolito Desideri left Rome for Lisbon with Grassi, who was destined for the mission of Mysore. They made first for Livorno, where they embarked on a coastal vessel that took them to Genoa. There on 22 November they boarded a ship bound for Lisbon. It was a long, stormy passage and they had to seek shelter along the coast in Barcelona, Alicante and Málaga. Here they had to wait for a favourable wind to carry them through the Straits of Gibraltar. At Cadiz, writes Desideri, 'we met with more trouble. A large Turkish ship lay out at sea waiting to attack us, so we cruised around and at length disembarked at Sesimbra,'some twenty miles south of Lisbon. The Jesuits finally reached that city in the middle of March 1713.

Very little time was spent in Lisbon. 'We embarked on 7 April,' Desideri continues,

> in one of the three ships bound for Goa and along with the fleet sailing to Brazil. We kept company with them for about ten days, then early in May we crossed the Line and became becalmed for some days. But soon we experienced what the Portuguese call trovadas, storms of short duration but very severe while they last. These drove us south of the Line and then, like all ships making for India, we sailed out into mid-Atlantic in order to gain a favourable wind that would take us past the Cape of Good Hope.
>
> At the end of June we passed the Cape and sailed towards the Mozambique Channel and arrived safely at the Isle of Mozambique on 25 July, three and a half months after leaving Lisbon.

At Mozambique there was a long delay until ships from Senna arrived bringing a consignment of large elephant tusks, gold, silver and black amber as well as a large number of Kaffir or Negro slaves destined for the market at Goa.

Crossing the Line again in early September, they sighted the Indian coast on the nineteenth of the same month. Three days later they disembarked at Goa. Writing to the General on November 15 after his arrival in India, Desideri said that he had been appointed to the mission of Tibet. He was delighted. But aware that opinion was still divided on the wisdom of re-entering the country, he took the unusual step of asking the General to address him a special letter confirming his appointment and ordering him explicitly to Tibet; at the same time he asked permission to act in all that concerned the mission under the direct authority of Rome: this no doubt was to enable him to overcome any objections to his enterprise that the Jesuits in Goa opposed to the mission might throw in his path.

After receiving his appointment Desideri had promptly left Goa on 13 November for Surat on the Gulf of Cambay, where he joined Fr Manuel Freyre, a Portuguese born in 1679 at Ancião, who was to be his Superior and travelling companion. On 11 May 1714 they reached Delhi. Here they had to wait four or five months on account of the rains: during this time Desideri learned a smattering of Persian, the common language of all traders in central Asia.

On 24 September that same year they set out for Lahore, which they reached on 9 October. Ten days later they left for Srinagar. Passing through Gujerat, they took the mountain road to Kashmir. 'These mountains,' writes Desideri,

> are like staircases piled up on top of one another; the highest point is called Pir Panjal after a tutelary spirit held in high honour by the people. The mountain is very high, steep and difficult. It is covered for several months by deep snow, while in the valleys there is ice, resembling marble in hardness, which never melts. Ice-cold torrents divide these mountains so that the road is always ascending and descending: this did not trouble me, but the continual wading through cold streams gave me dysentery with consequent loss of blood lasting nine months. Notwithstanding the altitude, the slopes of these mountains are pleasant enough with their fruit and other trees and different kinds of plants that grow everywhere. The inhabitants are governed by petty kings and there are caravanserais at the end of each stage for the convenience of travellers.

Having crossed the Pir Panjal Range, Desideri reached the town of Caximir, the present Srinagar, on 13 November.

Desideri gives a picturesque account of this historic capital of Kashmir, with its numerous canals, Buddhist ruins, and sixteenth-century fort built by Akbar the Great; it was one of the famed summer resorts of the East, with a thriving traffic in silk and shawls.

'You must know,' he writes,

that in the second Tibet the capital of which is six weeks' journey from Srinagar by a most precipitous road, there are untold numbers of sheep whose wool is pure white, very long and remarkably fine. The merchants of Kashmir keep a large number of agents in the Second Tibet. They collect the wool during the year, paying a most miserable price for it. From May to August thousands of men travelled between Srinagar and Leh, the capital of the Second Tibet, and return with heavy loads of this wool. In Kashmir it is spun into a very fine thread and then woven into the very delicate cashmere cloth that is renowned all over India.

When Desideri arrived in Kashmir, the first snows had already fallen and the road to Tibet was impassable. Forced to remain in Srinagar, the two priests rented a house. Although very ill with dysentery – he says he was almost at death's door – Desideri continued to study Persian; he had arrived with letters of introduction from the court at Lahore to the suba, the divan, and other nobles of Kashmir, who treated him with much honour.

On 13 May the priests were able to continue their journey. They now took with them an interpreter and three Christian servants, and they also carried passports and letters of recommendation for the King of Ladakh in east Kashmir on the border with China. Ladakh had nominally been a dependency of Tibet, but after 1531 it had been attacked and occupied by Muslim invaders.

Desideri had not been instructed to go to Lhasa, but to re-establish the Jesuit mission to Tibet. It is unlikely that he would have travelled through Kashmir and Ladakh had Lhasa been his goal.

Twelve days after leaving Srinagar, Desideri and his companion found themselves at the foot of a

steep, high and formidable mountain called Kastel, the summit of which is the boundary between Kashmir and Lesser Tibet, called by the inhabitants Baltistan. From the foot of Kastel it is a nine-month journey to China. . . . On 30 May, which was Ascension Day, we began the ascent of the mountain, which was covered with dense snow and hard ice. Heavy snow fell all through the day.

At night they came down to the first settlement, a hamlet called Matayanon on the other side of Mount Kastel. At this point in his narrative Desideri distinguishes 'three Tibets' and gives the boundaries and features of each. The second Tibet, consisting of the Kingdom of Ladakh, with its capital at Leh, he places between the district he was now entering and the region around Lhasa. The first Tibet, he says, was divided into small princedoms; it had no towns but only villages or hamlets with their houses half sunk into the ground; it produced barley, wheat, and some vegetables, but no fruit apart from apricots; until the recent Muslim incursions, the language and religion of the people had been the same as in the rest of Tibet. It was in this region that Desideri, like other priests before him, thought he could discern ancient traces of Buddhism in the religious practices of the people and in the ruins of numerous ancient lama monasteries, an observation which an early twentieth-century traveller confirmed.

No more than three days further on, the two Jesuits entered the second Tibet, the kingdom of Ladakh. This too was a predominantly Muslim area though ethnologically the people were more allied to the Tibetans. In the mid-nineteenth century this district was annexed to Kashmir and was later claimed by the Chinese, who in 1962 occupied part of it. Formerly made up of small kingdoms, this second Tibet was now governed from Leh, the capital. In this mountainous country Desideri found the inhabitants 'docile, polite, cheerful and kind'; trees and fuel were scarce, cattle plentiful, the population scant, and the trade consisted mainly of gold-bearing sand. There were numerous monasteries with large numbers of monks, all of whom lived under a chief lama.

It is not easy to trace the route followed by the two Jesuits to the capital Leh after they had entered the kingdom of Ladakh. Desideri says that the first places in this kingdom were ruled by a dependent Muslim prince. 'We sent him our letters of introduction,' writes Desideri,

> and begged him to let us pass freely through his dominions. He invited us to visit him the following morning, received us with much honour and many compliments, inviting us to dine with him. On the following day he returned our visit with a large retinue and much pomp and asked us to go with him

to watch an exhibition of cavalry exercises and games. Before we left the next day, he gave us not only the passports we had asked for but sent us some fine presents, some money for our servants and men to guide us safely over a perilous bridge on the way ahead.

Here Desideri writes of the same trepidation that all travellers, including the young Lord Curzon, have experienced while crossing rope bridges. As it was impossible to cross the rapid torrent either by wading or by swimming, Desideri's party were obliged to use a bridge of twisted willows.

Two thick ropes of willow are stretched nearly four feet apart, and hanging loops of smaller willow ropes about one and a half feet apart from each other are attached to them. A person must stretch out his arms and hold fast to the thicker ropes while placing one foot after the other into the hanging loops in order to reach the other side. With every step the bridge sways from left to right and from right to left, so that only one person can cross at a time. Besides this, one is so high above the river and the bridge is so open on all sides that the rush of water below dazzles the eyes and makes one dizzy.

After the priests had crossed the rope bridge, the guides left them. A few days later the travellers came to an important place where the son of Longbo, the first minister of Ladakh, was governor. When the governor heard of their arrival, he invited them to his palace, gave them some presents and sent them on with a letter of introduction to his father. The priests then pursued their journey to Leh, arriving there on 20 June 1715. Looking back on the hazards of their journey thus far, Desideri writes:

The journey from Kashmir to Leh, the capital of the second Tibet, which can only be accomplished on foot, takes forty days. The path is so narrow that we were obliged to go in single file. It leads up the side of very high and terrible mountains. In places the path had been destroyed by avalanches or by heavy rains and there was no foothold. Where that happened someone had to go ahead and cut a step the size of a man's foot with his axe and then, giving me his left hand, he would help me to put my foot into the step. He would

then cut another, and so on until we struck the narrow
path again. In other places the mountain was so
covered with ice and snow that the path became
extremely dangerous; should your foot slip, there was
nothing to stop you from falling headlong into the
torrent below.
Many of the men coming from Kashmir to collect sheep's wool,
Desideri was told, lost their lives or were crippled in this way. In
fact, one of his own servants slipped on the ice, fell, and rolled
down the mountain side; he was saved only because the load he
was carrying on his shoulders buried itself in the snow and
checked his fall. On their approach to Leh, Freyre narrates, they
spent a night in a mountain cave, as they frequently did. The next
morning Desideri's eyes began dripping water from the glare of the
sun on the snow, and he was unable to distinguish one person from
another in their party. Their Muslim carriers from Kashmir were
also suffering from snow blindness and demanded to be allowed to
return. Cajoled, however, to continue, they each tore a piece from
their worn tunic and rubbed it in the charcoal of their spent fire,
stretching it across their eyes like a veil. The two priests did the
same with their handkerchiefs, and then rubbed their eyes with
snow to reduce the glare. The land produced nothing and all provisions – rice, vegetables and butter – had to be carried by the men
in addition to their baggage.

'There are no large towns in this kingdom,' Desideri writes,
but only villages, farmsteads and castles, with the one
exception of Leh, the capital, where the King and the
chief lama of this kingdom live. This town, situated in
a wide plain entirely surrounded by mountains and
studded with villages, is built on the slope of a mountain and stretches up as far as the residence of the chief
lama and the palace of the King, both fine buildings.
The whole is crowned with a large fort close to the
summit, on which there is another fort. Below the fort
the town is encircled by walls and defended by gates.
His description follows closely that of travellers who visited Leh
more than a century later.

Leh at the time of Desideri's visit was also an important commercial centre. Merchants from Bhutan were sometimes seen bringing

with them well-bred horses, cotton goods and other merchandise. Some also came from the third Tibet by way of the great desert, bearing tea and tobacco, bales of silk, and other wares from China. The arrival of the two priests in the city immediately came to the attention of the King. Even before they had time to present their letters of introduction, he sent a messenger to invite them to his palace. He received them kindly as travellers from a far-off country and with the honours usually accorded to lamas and doctors of the law. Without referring to the letters the priests carried, the King promised them his protection and saw that they were treated in the same manner by the Great Lama and the chief minister. Desideri does not mention the King's name in his book, but in a letter to his friend, Fr Grassi, with whom he had travelled from Rome to Lisbon and on to Goa, he calls him Nima Nangial. He had occupied the throne since 1680 and died three years after Desideri's visit.

Both the King and his chief minister were eager to retain the two priests and have them practise as doctors of the law. Desideri had already begun to study the language intensely and hoped shortly 'to see some fruits pleasing to his Divine Majesty cropping up among the barren rocks of Tibet'. For three months he deliberated whether he should accept the King's invitation; in the end he decided to go on. He was anxious to enter the third Tibet, the centre of Lamaism. And there was a further reason for not remaining in Leh. The difficult journey from Kashmir had left Fr Freyre exhausted. He was advised that the least burdensome route home was via Lhasa.

'And so we left Leh,' Desideri writes, 'on 17 August 1715, and arrived at Lhasa on 18 March 1716.' On their departure the King provided the priests with horses, presents and passports to the local governors under his jurisdiction; they were also given letters to the lama, the governor and the castellan of a town called Tashigong.

For some days they rode with their guides through mountainous and uninhabited country until they entered a wide plain with pools of foul and sulphurous water. Here both men and horses suffered from violent swellings on the gums and lips that were usually healed by chewing herbs and garlic. This region was too high and too cold to be used for anything but pasture. There were no trees to be seen, only salt lakes scattered at intervals in the vast sterile flats.

When they had travelled for three weeks over this mountain plateau, on 7 September they entered the third Tibet at Tashigong, a town defended by strong walls and a deep ditch with draw-bridges. Thanks once more to their letters of introduction, they were kindly received by the lama. Desideri had been forewarned that the third Tibet was more exposed to the incursions of the Tartar tribes living on its borders than the other two Tibets.

The town of Tashigong lay at the edge of a vast desert that reportedly took three months to cross. The rulers of the city could find no guide to conduct them across; to attempt it alone was certain death.

Then unexpectedly they were offered the best escort they could have wished for. Two days' journey beyond Tashigong, in a large district called Gartok, a strong garrison of Tartar and Tibetan soldiers subject to the King of the Third Tibet was stationed not merely to defend Tashigong and the neighbouring villages but also to hold in check the armed brigands that terrorized the country-side.

A Tartar prince had been in charge of these troops, but on his death two years earlier their command had been taken over by his widow. She had obtained permission to return to Lhasa with her troops and had arranged for another contingent under another commander to take over the garrison. Early in October she came to Tashigong to complete arrangements for the formation of the caravan. 'We were presented to her,' writes Desideri, 'and begged to be allowed to travel under her protection to Lhasa. With most kind words the princess replied that she would do all in her power to help us and to make the long and difficult journey as pleasant as possible. She added that she esteemed it a great honour to be allowed to assist two lamas from a distant land.'

While waiting in their tent in the plain, Freyre records, 'the cold was so intense that one day when Fr Ippolito was washing in the river, raising the water to his face with his cupped hands, it actually froze on his beard; he looked a fine sight with all the icicles adorning it.'

On 9 October the priests left Tashigong and two days later arrived at Gartok, where they waited for additions to the caravan. It was after leaving Tashigong that Freyre, finding the cold almost unendurable, was comforted by the Tartar princess with hot tea and some meat. 'Once,' he writes, 'she saw me frozen to a state of inertia and ordered her servants to bring her some goatskins. "Hand me your coat," she said, and commanded a servant to line the sleeves with the goatskins, placing the fur inside to keep my hands warm.'

About the middle of the month they set out finally for Lhasa, a journey no European after Desideri was to undertake until 1904. At the head of the caravan rode a number of the princess's servants and squadrons of Tartar cavalry, followed by the princess herself and some Tartar ladies, all on horseback; then came her ministers and the officers of her army, followed by more Tartar cavalry with whom the priests usually rode; the rear-guard was composed of still more cavalry, partly Tartar, partly Tibetan, and finally the baggage train, the provisions, a crowd on foot and some others leading horses.

On 9 November they reached what Desideri describes as 'the highest region we have traversed during the whole of our peregrinations.' He continues:

> It is a complete desert called Ng-nari Giogar and is held in the highest veneration on account of a certain Urghien, the founder of the Tibetan religion. Away from the road stands an enormously high mountain, very wide in circumference, its summit hidden among the clouds and covered with perpetual snow and ice: it is horrible, barren and bitterly cold. In a cave of that mountain, according to the legend, lived Urghien in absolute retirement and uninterrupted meditation. In his honour this cave has been changed into a temple. Not only do the Tibetans visit the cave, invariably leaving some presents, but with very great inconvenience to themselves, they circuit the whole mountain, which takes them several days. Doing this they gain what I might call indulgences[or what a twentieth-century writer describes as protection from evil] for the rest of their years.

This is the first account by a European of one of the most sacred shrines of Buddhist Tibet. The mountain is Kailas or Kang-Rinpoche, 22,028 feet high, the seat of the gods of the religious world of central Asia. It is visited by pilgrims from the Tibetan uplands and the Himalayan fastnesses. Urghien, whose seat is here, is better known by his Indian name, Padmasambhava, the Lotus-eater. The founder of Lamaism, he was given the name Urghien because he came from Urgyan, the district north of Peshawar. The mountain stands in isolation from the Himalayan Range. It is the dearest aspiration of every devout Buddhist and Hindu to visit it once at least in a lifetime. Pilgrims fast and live on alms during their journey, and when they come in sight of the mountain they prostrate themselves and add a stone to the cairn which marks these places on the roads that converge on the mountain.

'Owing to the snow on this mountain,' writes Desideri, 'my eyes became so inflamed that once again I almost lost my sight. I had no spectacles, and the only remedy, as I learned from the escort, was to rub the eyes with snow.' Freyre, riding at the end of the caravan, was again in danger. In the sharp cold his horse began to bleed from the nostrils, then to stagger from hunger; towards nightfall it sank dead in the snow. Falling behind the caravan with only a Muslim servant near him, Freyre lost sight of the others as darkness fell. All he could do to protect himself from the cold was to lie that night close to the dead horse's belly. Desideri, in another part of the caravan, noticing his companion's absence, informed the princess that he was missing. 'The lady,' writes Freyre, 'drew me back from the claws of death, sending me grooms with three horses and with food to revive me. On the next day she made me the gift of another saddle horse, and so we left that place with nothing ahead of us but open snow-fields.'

Continuing across the plateau, on 1 December they reached a sandy plain that Desideri calls Toscioa, on which roamed goats, sheep and yaks belonging to the Grand Lama and to the King of Tibet. Here they rested their men and horses for two days. All around were tents of the shepherds who rove across the desert pasturing their herds of horses, mules, and mountain cows. A short distance further on, they came to a settlement called Retoa close by the sacred lake of Manasarovar, famous in Hindu mythology and a place of pilgrimage. 'It is known, I may say, over the entire world,' writes Desideri, 'that on the shores and sands of this lake large quantities of gold dust are found. . . . Tibetan and other merchants come to the lake from time to time in search of gold.'

Then for several more weeks they rode on through a desertlike and forlorn region that in its surrounding hills produced large quantities of gold. The area was not under cultivation and there were no villages, only numerous herds that produced excellent butter.

On 4 January 1716, leaving the barren country behind, they came to a large well-fortified town called Ser-kla, the residence of the governor and chief of the province of Zang-to. Here the Tartar princess was taken ill. Unable to continue alone, the priests were delayed here until 28 January. At last they resumed their journey and reached Shigatse, where they stayed for a few days. Finally, as Desideri calculates, two years and four months after leaving Goa, and one and a half years after leaving Delhi, and ten whole months after leaving Kashmir, they arrived on 18 March 1716 at Lhasa, which they now decided should be the site of the new mission.

It is only when they had reached the capital that Desideri reflected on the hardships of his journey: the difficulties of obtaining food, the want of fuel, life in a tent, the unbearable cold, the difficult tracks through snow and ice, the care of the horses (between Lek and Lhasa alone they lost seven horses). 'Often crossing mountain torrents,' Desideri wrote to his friend Fr Grassi, 'I had to cling to the tail of an ox to prevent myself from being carried away by the force of the currents.'

Although all this is no different from the descriptions of modern travel in Tibet, Desideri and his companion were ignorant of mountain travel and had no previous experience of its difficulties and hazards. Writers on Tibet have invariably stressed how much more arduous travel in these regions becomes as winter sets in. From the second half of October until the middle of March, the two Jesuits had suffered and survived the severity of the mountain winter. For Fr Freyre the journey proved too much: with a constitution already weakened by many years in the tropics, he was unable to acclimatize himself to the thin air and extreme cold of the Himalayas. On reaching Lhasa he rested for a short time and then made his way back to Hindustan, taking the more frequented road through Nepal.

Rather more than fifty years earlier, Grueber and d'Orville had passed through Lhasa. Grueber had sketched the Potala but had little to say about the city. Desideri was told that Lhasa was originally the name of a temple built on the site of the city; he noted that it had a large mixed population of Tartars, Chinese, Muscovites and Armenians from Kashmir, Hindustan and Nepal who traded daily in the large central square, the site of a fair held daily from early morning to sundown. Almost all the finer houses, which were three or four storeys high, had their own chapel; the rooms were spacious and comfortable with floors made of a kind of mosaic that gleamed like a mirror; there was a room set aside as an oratory where lamps burned in front of images of the gods with offerings of fruit in front of them. The owners of these houses usually lived on the top floor, letting out the rooms in the rest of the house. He observed that the city could easily be defended thanks to four narrow valleys opening onto the broad plain where it was situated.

Desideri's is the only description of the central square at this period. 'On the west side of this square,' he writes,

> stands an ancient and very rich temple called Lha-Brang, or Palace of the Lha. In the porch are fine pictures. Within there are many recesses like chapels that are dedicated to the different gods of these people. . . . Like other temples of Tibet, it has a flat roof. From this roof rise a number of pillars supporting a canopy made of bronze or brass plates ornamented with bas reliefs, the whole being beautifully gilded. . . . Daily services in the temple are conducted by a large number of monks who live in a vast monastery close by. . . . The temple is surrounded by a wide street, and it is along this street that Tibetans make their khora or circuit of the temple in such a way as to have the building always on their right, thus securing a great remission of punishment. No one, not even the king, may pass through this street on horseback.

Freyre's departure left Desideri the only European in Lhasa. Desideri had been in the city a very short time when he was summoned to the palace by command of the King and was cross-examined by his commander-in-chief, Zze-ring-tong-drup, on the purpose of his visit. About four weeks later, on 1 May, he was received in audience by the King seated on his throne. This was Cinghes Khan, the grandson of Guchi Khan, the chief of the Tartars of Koko-Nor, who had conquered Tibet in 1641. Desideri is quick to point out that the King was then no more than the deputy of the Dalai Lama, who was an absolute ruler. It was in the Dalai Lama's name that the King administered civil, criminal, and military affairs. 'But the Dalai Lama,' Desideri writes after visiting him in early July, 'is continually receiving visits and is frequently occupied discussing matters with the King, the nobles, the lamas, the heads of monasteries, with pious persons and even with merchants.' When Desideri saw him, he was in the company of other lamas, one of whom was the son of the Lompo or chief magistrate, another a close relation of the King.

The young Jesuit who was received with much courtesy both by the King and the Dalai Lama must have made a very favourable impression, because he was given permission to preach. He was also allowed to buy a house in the city: this was an exceptional favour, since foreigners were only permitted to rent lodgings. The King and others of his court, Desideri explains, regarded him as a lama of the law of Jesus Christ from the Western world. 'They often say, "If only we knew your language or you ours, we would so much like you to explain your religion."'

Promptly Desideri bought a house in the centre of Lhasa in the main street, the Khorap. 'From that day to the last which I passed in the kingdom,' he wrote, 'I made it a rule to study from early morning till sundown, and for nearly six years took nothing during the day save tea to drink; the only exceptions were feast days and some extraordinary occasions.'

During this period Desideri received daily a messenger from the King enquiring what progress he had made with the language. On one occasion the messenger informed him that both the King and his viceroy had been taken seriously ill, which he ascribed to the delayed effect of an attempt to poison them. Desideri happened to have by his bed a vase of Roman teriaca, a drug already in use in imperial Rome, containing fifty-seven ingredients tested by prolonged use. Desideri sent the vase to the King. Both the King and his viceroy slept well that night and were in good health the next morning.

Meanwhile, three and a half months earlier, on 1 October 1716, rather more than six months after Desideri's arrival, a party of three Capuchin friars arrived in the capital via Nepal. Desideri welcomed them into his house and helped them to learn the language.

Some ten years previous to their arrival, other Capuchins had reached Lhasa by the same route but had left in disappointment soon afterwards.

It appears that after the failure of the first Jesuit mission in Tibet, the country had been handed over to the Capuchin friars, without knowledge of the Pope, by the newly created department for the missions, known as the Congregation for the Propagation of the Faith (Propaganda); Tibet was to be reserved to the Capuchins as a mission area to the total exclusion of priests of any other religious order. Desideri, however, rightly considered that he had the Pope's authorization to re-establish the Jesuit mission in the country, and that this was also the mind of the Jesuits both in Rome and in Goa. While waiting for the Capuchins to obtain a copy of the decree issued them by Propaganda, Desideri continued with his studies.

By the end of December 1617, nine months after his arrival in Lhasa, Desideri had completed a short exposition of Christian belief in Tibetan and a month later presented it to the King, who advised him to study the religion of the lamas in their own writings. Accordingly Desideri went daily from his house to the monastery of Ramo-cce in the city. There, to use his own words, he 'read or rather devoured' the more important books of the *Kaa-n-ghiur* (The Translated Commandment), so called because it was a translation from the ancient Indian language and in some cases from the Chinese, containing 1,083 distinct works collected in some 115 books.

In August 1717 Desideri, acting again on the advice of the King, moved for deeper study to the university of Sara, a short distance from Lhasa, where lamas came from all parts of Tibet, Tartary and China to pursue higher studies. Here he was allotted comfortable quarters and an oratory where he was able to say Mass; he was also given the use of the university libraries and was able to hold discussions with the professors. 'This university,' Desideri writes,

> is situated about two miles from Lhasa. Its great walls,
> its streets, squares, palaces and two large temples,
> together with a population of thousands of monks,
> make it almost a town in itself. Moreover, on the slope
> of the mountain against which it is built are a number
> of hermitages for those who want to pass some time
> in solitude. East of Sara on another mountain lies a

nunnery, and between the two mountains runs the road to Dam, where the eastern desert begins. The monastic community at Sara consisted of three colleges or 'residences of learning': the first college was given over to the study of elementary monastic principles and ritual, the second to more elevated studies, and the third to esoteric and mystical doctrine and practice. All three communities met daily in the great assembly hall, which served as a temple for the whole community; here the walls were covered with brilliant parti-colored frescoes and scrolls hung from verandahs and pillars. On the roof of the temple was a summer house used by the Dalai Lama. Some of the more accomplished lamas were trained as painters, others were taught calligraphy, carving and embroidery, while the less gifted were put to domestic tasks. Each house that made up the college had fifty or sixty monks living in small cells. None had any private possessions apart from a butter lamp and an ikon. On entering as children, all were given the red cowl that they wore for the rest of their lives. Most did not pass beyond the first college, whereas the higher grade with whom Desideri consorted had studied the teaching of Buddha for thirty or forty years. Some, after passing their final examination, might be permitted to become hermits. Since only Tibetans and Mongolians were permitted to join the monastery, the privilege granted Desideri by the King was quite exceptional.

There were distinct classes of hermits as well as of monks. Among the different schools or classes, the most respected were the ascetics vowed to perpetual silence; they lived sometimes in caves with a small opening through which food and oil for their lamps could be passed. Unlike the monks, they usually had beards. Others were mendicants or wandering monks; and there were still others who professed magic and made a living by it.

Here at the university Desideri worked in its famous library, learned the principal Tibetan dialects, and held discussions with the monks, principally with the doctors and teachers. 'Above all,' he writes, 'I attempted to understand those most abstruse, subtle and intricate treatises called *Tongba-gni* or *Vacuum*, which are to be taken not in a material or philosophical way but in an intellectual and mystical sense.' These books dealt with religious ceremonial and their accompanying apparatus of bells, cups, and offerings.

Determined to extract the meaning of these abstruse books

containing the core of Tibetan doctrine, Desideri read attentively and made enquiries but received no help from the doctors. 'I read, reread,' he wrote, 'and studied until, thanks be to God, I not only understood but completely mastered all the subtle, sophisticated, and abstruse matter that was so necessary and important for me to know.'

Alongside this probe into doctrinal niceties, Desideri examined the differences between Christian and Tibetan contemplation. In his judgement, Tibetan contemplation, which was governed by rigid rules, put too much emphasis on its benefits and its absolute necessity. 'They divide it,' he wrote, 'into ordinary meditation, immobile and fixed contemplation, and a more subtle and absorbed elevation of the spirit that raises a man above himself, above all visible things, above the earth and above all humanity.' Desideri, in this first study of Tibetan contemplation by a European, judged that when they were practising its highest form, the monks were deceiving themselves; for they held that a man 'disappears even to himself and that to a cleansed and purified mind all things vanish and nothing exists.'

Tibetan fasting served much the same ends as did the Christian practice. While at Sara Desideri conformed to the rule of the monks, who in their fasts ate only in the evening and took only a little liquid in the course of the day. The laity also fasted three or four times a month. On these days they offered up sacrifices, employed monks to say prayers in their homes and gave alms to the poor; the women indicated that they were fasting by wearing no jewels or finery. Although not certain on this point, Desideri thought that one of these fast days was on the tenth day of the moon in honour of Urghien, who had introduced religion into Tibet.

Prayers for the dead were indeed said, as the first Jesuits to enter the country had observed. On death the soul passed for seven days into a state known as *parto*, then left for a reincarnation into one of three states that were the reward for virtue; it was at this stage that prayers were valued. 'They do not admit,' Desideri writes in an especially interesting passage, 'that the soul enters the body when the embryo attains a sufficient organization, but declare that the soul enters at the very moment of conception.'

Desideri had scarcely begun to write when his work was interrupted by a national disaster. The country was invaded by a vast horde of Tartars from Sungaria, between the highlands of Mongolia and the lowlands of Turkestan. By nature marauders, they advanced to Si-ning in the Chinese province of Kansu under their chieftain Tse Wang. From Si-ning Tse Wang dispatched his brother to Lhasa, leading a force of sixty thousand. They had no difficulty in routing a much smaller and ill-equipped Tibetan army that attempted to bar its way to the capital at Tengrilate to the east of the Sara monastery.

The horde reached Lhasa on 3 December. The King with his son and his ministers escaped through a secret passage. Closely pursued, the King was caught and murdered after his horse stumbled. For two days Lhasa was given over to pillage. The Dalai Lama's new palace on Potala Hill was sacked along with temples and monasteries in the city and in several small towns in the district. Desideri's house in the city where the Capuchins were residing did not escape. 'Had I not seen it with my own eyes,' he writes, 'I would not have believed it, but no sooner had the Chinese penetrated into Tibet than the country flowed with silver. To supply his needs, every soldier had received advanced payment for five years in pieces of uncoined silver of various sizes. The Tibetans were at a loss how to dispose of this abundance and sent most of it to Nepal to exchange it by weight for the currency of that country, a transaction which brought the Nepalese a handsome profit.'

In order to continue his writing in comparative safety, Desideri retired to the hamlet of Trong-g-nee in the province of Takpo-Khier, eight days' journey from Lhasa. Here he remained from late 1717 or early 1718 to April 1721, with the exception of a short stay of three months in Lhasa, where he was able to give his book to his former Tibetan teacher, requesting his comments.

He found the Tibetans of the countryside a likeable people and was soon on easy terms with them, aided by his present facility in the language: he has a long section in his narrative on its symbols, thirty in number, its vowels and consonants, its pronunciation and spelling. The language, he says, would not be so difficult if they did not write before, behind, above and below the character which they pronounce, and before other characters which they do not pronounce; the difficulty is further increased by each of their four vowels having a fourfold value.

Living close to the Tibetans, Desideri came to admire their acute

minds and their lively, cheerful and industrious disposition. He
found that everyone could usefully employ himself in some way or
another, even if it was only in spinning, weaving or rope-making.
He made a list of fourteen industries and discovered in the course
of his research that the true artisans were rarely skilled in just one
craft. Their painting and sculpture, though passable, were not of
the highest order; they were proficient, however, in casting statues,
vases and musket barrels.

The country where he was now living remained a *terra incognita*
to travellers well into the nineteenth century. 'There are two places
of importance in the Takpo district,' he writes, in a fascinating
description of a monastic enclave that offers points of comparison
with Mount Athos:

> One is a rugged, high mountain with a plateau half
> way up. On it stands a splendid temple which is held
> in such high veneration by the people that both men
> and women come to live as hermits up and down the
> mountainside, some in monasteries, others in hermit-
> ages. Two palaces are residences of two lamas, one of
> whom belongs to the class which is permitted to
> marry in order to secure the succession, while the
> other has to remain single and will be succeeded by a
> reincarnate lama. The summit of the mountain con-
> sists of many clefts and crags; on one of them stands a
> building which serves as a retreat for the lamas and is
> connected with other crags by long wooden bridges.
> Many come to this place to present their offerings and
> to make arrangements for their bodies to be carried
> there after death, to be devoured by eagles and ravens.

'The other place of importance,' Desideri continues,

> is a wide tract of very high and wild mountains that
> form a kind of stairway. These two places are con-
> stantly visited by crowds of pilgrims who make their
> circuit there. The women, however, are permitted to
> climb only the lower mountains and are forbidden to
> cross a certain boundary under pain of death at the
> hands of the Khaa-n-dro-ma, a kind of guardian spirit.
> The men, however, may climb to any height they like
> but must observe certain rules on their ascent.

These mountains are covered with ice and snow on their summit all through the year. Several pilgrims perish there, but they think themselves happy to be allowed to die in this way. Even in these forlorn regions, hermits are found living here and there, and they are sought out by pilgrims.

During his long stay in the hamlet in the district of Trong-g-nee, Desideri was able to gather information about the neighbouring province of Lho-ro. 'On the south,' he writes, 'Trong-g-nee borders on the so-called Lhoba peoples, with whom they carry on trade, but very cautiously, for they consist of exceedingly savage tribes.' The Lhobas, he explains,

> live mostly in woods and in wretched cabins, and their only occupation is hunting every kind of game, the flesh of which is eaten raw or ill roasted. They sometimes feed on human flesh and do not scruple to kill a man when he appears to be healthy and plump. They always go armed with bow and arrow and are excellent archers. One very barbarous custom obtains among them: when a man sees a kinsman or beloved friend at the point of death, he consoles him in his extremity with the promise that he shall not leave the world alone; he undertakes to give him such and such a number of companions, mentioning a specific number. If the man dies, he kills the number stated; and as an authentic proof of the faithful discharge of his promise, he wears a collar of as many teeth as he has killed men.

'These people,' Desideri continues,

> do not allow anyone to travel through their country, no matter who the stranger may be, and for this reason they watch the roads and keep them in an impassable condition. . . . But even their neighbours and trading friends, the Tibetans of Congbo, are not permitted to cross the frontier; they bring there their merchandise, which consists chiefly of large quantities of excellent yellow and white honey, wax, cinnamon, cardamon and many other medical herbs.

This is close to a first-hand account of these savage people, for

Desideri concludes his description, saying in his usual matter-of-fact manner, that he had been within half a day's journey of their country. He was the first traveller of any nation to report on them. In 1874 Naim Singh on his march down the valley of Dirang was overtaken by a party of fifteen of them. He was struck by the enormous development of their arms and calves; they wore cylindrical hats made of bamboos and their only clothing was a long blanket folded like a Scotch plaid and fastened round the waist with a cloth girdle which served also as a quiver for their arrows; over their shoulder they slung a bow; they wore no boots. Their high cheekbones and narrow eyes made them resemble the Chinese. They lived by hunting, leaving the cultivation of the soil to their womenfolk.

The climate of Tibet appears to have suited Desideri. Out in the country he found the people to be generally healthy, but in the towns many suffered from venereal disease, for which they had excellent short-term cures. As soon as a man fell ill a *Ccio-Kiong*, a kind of sorcerer or lama, was summoned to determine which doctor should be consulted. If the patient got worse under his treatment, a band of monks would be summoned to hold a *corim*; this consisted in making offerings while prayers were sung to the accompaniment of musical instruments. For the rest of the day there would be readings aloud from one of the sacred books; this might go on for one or two or even more days. If the patient could afford it, money was sent to one of the monasteries to have a *corim* held there. If the patient recovered, another *corim* was held in thanksgiving.

An insuperable obstacle to their acceptance of Christianity, in Desideri's view, was the fairly common practice of polyandry. If the husband had younger brothers, each of them took his sister-in-law as his wife, and together they formed a single family. The children belonged to the eldest brother and were treated as nephews or nieces by the other brothers. Desideri ascribes this custom to two factors: the poor quality of the soil, which would not support a family if the land were parcelled out; secondly, the shortage of women. When the bride was conducted to the bridegroom's house, she made a show of resisting with all her strength, keeping up the fiction that she had been married against her consent. Looking perhaps once more at the possibility of bringing their customs into line with Catholic law, Desideri explained that no marriages were permitted among the descendants of the same father at any remove, adding that affinity as a rule created no impediment beyond the first degree.

Still further removed from any Christian character were the Tibetan funeral practices. Desideri describes more fully than most later writers the different ways of disposing of the bodies of the dead, depending upon the rank or wealth of the mourners. As in the case of sickness, the sorcerer had a part to play, for his advice was usually sought and followed. In the case of people of wealth, position or property, he would order cremation, which was always costly in a country where fuel was hard to obtain. Those less well-off might carry the corpse to the summit of a holy mountain and there dismember it and leave it to the eagles and vultures: this was the common treatment for monks. Those who had no money took the body to a certain spot called Tur-tro, where it was cut into small pieces as food for the dogs that wandered in the wild.

Desideri does not accept the view that the custom of leaving the dead to wild beasts reflected their belief that it was the highest honour to have a last resting place in the belly of a living creature. The reason for the practice, he says, is quite different: namely, they regarded the gift of oneself as food to others as the most sublime expression of sympathy with all living creatures. Since it was more than could be asked of a person to make this gift in one's lifetime, the offering was put off until death. In this way also the person returned into the cycle of innumerable transmigrations.

While gathering information about the country, Desideri was at the same time working on his book for the Christian instruction of the people. He divided his treatise into three volumes. The first argued against the transmigration of souls in Buddhist theology, the second against the denial of an absolute Being, the uncreated Creator of the world. The third volume offered an exposition of Christian teaching in the form of a dialogue between a Buddhist and a Christian. The book aroused great interest. 'My house,' Desideri wrote, 'suddenly became the scene of incessant comings and goings by all sorts of people, but chiefly by learned men and professors who came from the monasteries and the universities . . . to ask permission to see and read the book.'

A tireless writer, whether living at Lhasa or at Sara or in the

Takpo country, Desideri was always gathering material for a wide-ranging survey of the country, its system of justice, local government, defence organization, its climate, customs and the character of the people. He provided a comprehensive study perhaps unsurpassed to this day, which Sven Hedin acknowledges to be not just the first trustworthy description of Tibet by a European but a work that will always remain a classic.

While Desideri was on a visit to Lhasa from the hamlet at Trong-g-nee in April 1791, a Capuchin Father showed him the decree of the Congregation of Propaganda under date of 1704. It assigned the mission of Tibet to his Order of Friars to the exclusion of every other religious Order, and explicitly to the exclusion of the Jesuits. This decree was a step toward implementing Propaganda's overall aim of wresting from the Crown of Portugal the rights that it had hitherto exercised over the missions in its dominions. In other regions apart from India, and particularly in China, the congregation had acted peremptorily without notifying either the Jesuit authorities or the Pope. Desideri could rightly claim that he had received from Clement XI himself permission to enter Tibet.

At the same time as Desideri was confronted with the decree of Propaganda, he received a letter from his Superior at Goa enclosing a letter from Michele Tamburini, the Jesuit General, ordering him to return to India. 'When I gave you permission to enter the kingdom of Tibet,' he wrote, 'I did not know that this mission had been assigned to the Capuchin Fathers. In fact, I supposed that since that mission had been founded by our Fathers who worked there until 1650 when they were expelled by a persecution, it had not been refounded by others.'

On 12 December 1718 Propaganda had sent an order to Tamburini to remove all Jesuits working in Tibet. Within days, certainly before the end of the year, the General had passed these orders on to Goa. As there was no certainty that the letter would reach Goa, he repeated his instructions in a letter dated 16 January 1719.

'When in Lhasa on 16 April 1721,' writes Desideri, 'the Capuchin Fathers showed me the decree of the Holy Congregation of Propaganda bestowing on them the exclusive right to the mission in the kingdom of Tibet, I immediately obeyed and left Lhasa on 28 January with the Capuchin, the Reverend Father Giuseppe Felice.'

The usual route from Lhasa to Kuti on the Nepalese border lay

through Shigatse and Sakya, but because of the disturbed state of
the country after the change of government, Desideri in company
with Fr Felice took the more difficult road by way of Gyantse.

'On this journey,' Desideri writes,

> one passes a very high and testing mountain called
> Langur. Everyone who crosses it will infallibly feel
> great discomfort, especially a severe headache, short-
> ness of breath, and difficulty in breathing; in addition
> to this, some are affected by fever, as indeed I was
> during the whole day it took to cross the mountain
> and the night we spent on it. Though it was the end of
> May, the snow was still very deep and the cold so
> extreme and the wind so piercing that in spite of my
> thick clothing I was quite numbed and feared that I
> would not live through it. The common remedy
> against the discomforts of mountaineering is to chew
> roasted rice or sugar candy, or cloves, cinnamon and a
> species of Indian nut the Portuguese call *arecca*. As it is
> impossible to cross the Langur in a single day, a large
> house has been built where travellers can pass the
> night. But is so difficult to breathe that many find it
> impossible to stay indoors and have to sleep in the
> open. . . . There are many people who think that these
> difficulties may be due to volatilizing minerals hidden
> in the mountain; but as no trace of them has so far
> been found, I am inclined to ascribe these phenomena
> to the extremely thin and keen air. I am more inclined
> to believe this because my chest and breathing became
> worse when I met the wind on top of Langur and also
> because many people were more affected inside the
> house where the air is made thinner by the fire than
> when sleeping in the open air. It would have been the
> reverse had the sickness been caused by exhalations
> from the minerals or by pestilential vapours from the
> earth.

Curiously, some later travellers ascribed these conditions to the
action of carbonic acid.

After thirty-two days of travel on horseback from early morning
to sunset with only an hour's rest at midday to drink tea and eat

something, the two priests arrived at Kuti or Nilam Dzong on 30 May 'Knowing that it was dangerous to leave Tibet at this time of the year for Nepal,' writes Desideri, 'I decided to remain until the winter at Kuti.' He explains that during the summer months influenza is prevalent in Katmandu and takes a heavy toll of the inhabitants. He therefore took an apartment in a house belonging to a notable of the town and awaited the approach of winter.

At Kuti, as he wrote Desideri 'reflected that, notwithstanding my prompt obedience to the decree of Propaganda, it was not well absolutely to cede the rights that the Society of Jesus had over the mission [to Tibet], so I sent from Kuti to Rome an appeal with faithful and full information on the mission.' His letters were addressed to Propaganda, to the Pope and to the General of the Society. He complained bitterly that the Superior of the Capuchins, Fr Domenico de Fana, had protested so vehemently that he could not tolerate the presence of a Jesuit in the mission and had begged the Pope to order the return of the Jesuits. He felt confident that his plea would be heard by Clement XI, who had blessed and approved of his departure.

Living in his apartment, Desideri became friendly with 'three governors of the town' and received much kindness from them.

'I might have left Kuti in November,' he writes, ' but hearing that a Capuchin friar, Fr Felice of Montvecchio, was expected from Lhasa, I waited till he arrived on 8 December, and on the fourteenth we set out together for Katmandu.' He continues:

> Although I enjoyed Fr Felice's amusing and interesting conversation, it pained me to see this man, now sixty years old, obliged to face the dangerous roads and bitter cold. Two or three days after leaving Kuti, we arrived at a place called Nesti [Listi], which seemed to be situated on the border between the two kingdoms; for half the inhabitants were subject to Lhasa, while the other half paid allegiance to Katmandu. In the course of the journey from Kuti to Katmandu . . . the road skirted frightful precipices, and there were places where we had to climb the mountain by cutting out the rock like a staircase and making holes just large enough to hold one's toes. At one point we crossed a chasm by a plank just

wide enough for a man's foothold, while the wooden bridges spanning the rivers in the deep valleys swayed and oscillated alarmingly.

During the last days of this journey we climbed one mountain after another; they were not so bare as in Tibet: there were grass and also some trees that gave us a little shade. In this type of country, it is impossible to ride, but there is no difficulty in finding men who will carry you: they have leather straps across the shoulders and forehead and attached to a board two hands in length and one hand in width. One sits on this board with legs hanging down and arms around the man's neck. Fr Felice, old and tired as he was, insisted on walking with me until at last I persuaded him to be carried; but this proved difficult, because he was so tall and heavy and it was hard to find anyone to carry his weight. He suffered a great deal.

They arrived at Katmandu on 27 December 1721.

Although Desideri's main interest was in Tibet, his long book covers the political organization of Nepal with its three royal cities Katmandu, Patan and Bhatgaon, and the character, religion, language and dress of the Nepalese. Unique among travellers in Nepal, Desideri studied the incidence of influenza: his fear that he might contract the infection had held him back at Kuti for the summer. He says that it is called *ol* in the country. The disease, he says, is not contracted in the mountains but at night, owing to the foul evaporations of stagnant water: the vapours arise during the day to come down again on every valley and plain during the night. The disease is practically incurable except by native remedies that are a tightly guarded secret; they have a drink called *bhang* made from dry leaves, possibly hemp or something like it, but in spite of this many die of the disease.

On 14 January Desideri left Katmandu for Bagao. Then he continued his journey in company with a Capuchin Father and an escort provided by the ruler. For many days they climbed and came down from mountains until they reached a plain which was the boundary between Nepal and Bettiah. Dismissing the escort provided by the ruler of Bagao, they reached a place on the plain called Posse that was part of the kingdom of Bettiah.

'On our way from there,' Desideri writes,

we came to two wide rivers; the first we crossed on the back of our men, the second in a boat. There was a third river, which again we crossed by boat before we reached Messi [Maisi], where we were taken to the custom-house in the main square to have everything we carried minutely examined. This is a large, populous, rich city subject to the Mogul emperor. . . . Finally we arrived safely in Singeah and were most kindly and magnificently received by a Dutchman, Gerard Pelgrom, who worked for the Dutch East India Company. The Capuchin Fathers of Patna came to meet us and on 6 February all of us, including Gerard Pelgrom, floated down the river Gandatti, crossed the Ganges, and arrived happily at Patna, where I enjoyed the hospitality of the Capuchin Fathers in their hospice.

Passing through Patna, Benares, and Allahabad, Desideri reached Agra on 22 April 1722. Here he fell seriously ill. When he had recovered sufficiently to travel, he went for convalescence to Delhi, where he stayed until 1725. His few lines covering his stay there reveal something of his charm that made him such a welcome guest on his travels:

The church in Delhi was old, in bad repair and far too small, so I decided to build a larger and finer church. It was finished on the eve of All Saints' Day, 1723. . . . As the people there are fond of gardens, I made one in front of my house by the church with trees for shade and all my best-loved flowers. . . . I kept my front door and the door of my study open all day until nightfall, welcomed all who came, listened to them patiently, and composed their quarrels.

While there, Desideri was instructed to make his way to Europe. Offered a passage as chaplain by the governor-general of French East India on a ship bound for Brittany, he sailed from Pondicherry on 21 January.

On 29 April we sighted the Isle of St Helena, belonging to Britain; and as provisions were short, we decided to make for the Isle of Ascension, which we reached on May 7. There we anchored under a moun-

tain with a cross on its summit. The sailors killed a
great number of starlings, knocking them down with
sticks and even catching them in their hands. They
also captured fifty sea tortoises which come out of the
sea in the evening to lay their eggs in the sand: they
make excellent soup and their flesh is said to be an
excellent preservative against scurvy. All of us, nearly
two hundred persons, lived on these turtles with a
little bread and biscuit for the rest of the voyage.
On leaving Ascension Island on 9 May with a light breeze over a
calm sea, the ship was rammed at midnight and had her bow cut
away. Fortunately the damage was above the waterline. 'Believing
that they had been attacked by a privateer,' writes Desideri,

for there were five other ships not far away, they
manned the cannon, dismantled the cabins to make
room for the artillery, distributed arms and prepared
for battle. Some shots were fired by the ship that had
struck us, but they were only to call others to her assistance, for she also had been severely damaged in the
collision. After a close examination of our ship, the
captain decided to sail on, but judged it safer to make
first for South America, where the bow could be
repaired. On 11 June they cast anchor at Port St Pierre.
Leaving two weeks later, eventually, on 11 August,
they cast anchor in the royal harbor of Port Louis in
Lower Brittany.

Desideri reached Rome on 23 January 1728. Here he completed his
Notizie Istoriche del Tibet, and here he died at the age of forty-nine on
4 April 1733.

—◆◆◆—

Meanwhile, in 1719 four more Capuchins had reached Lhasa, travelling from Patna via Nepal, and had established a mission there.
The goodwill of the Dalai Lama, assiduously cultivated by Desideri, was extended to the friars. In 1724 they were given permission
to build a chapel, where from time to time the Dalai Lama would
visit them and hold discussions on religious subjects. In 1740 the
Dalai Lama received formal greetings from Pope Clement XII.

For another twenty years the Capuchins remained in the city, until they were expelled under pressure from the Chinese Resident. Settling eventually with their Christian converts at Bettiah in Bengal on the borders of Tibet, they were among the first victims of the policy to exclude foreigners that was rigorously enforced throughout the nineteenth century. Typical of several others, spies and adventurers, who then attempted to penetrate Tibet was Colonel Waddell. In 1892, in the disguise of a Tibetan pilgrim, he set out in the usual manner with surveying instruments secreted in a prayer wheel, a hollow walking stick, and a flat-bottomed basket. Like the rest, however, he failed to penetrate the tightly guarded frontiers. To escape detection was impossible for a European, because it was the responsibility of the headman of every village to identify foreigners attempting to enter the country. Twice Sven Hedin failed to reach Lhasa. In 1893, disguised as a Buriat Mongol and escorted by four Cossacks, he succeeded in getting as fas as a villa some hundred and fifty miles northwest of the capital.

Not until 1904, when Captain Younghusband marched on Lhasa and Sven Hedin's writings on central Tibet excited worldwide interest in the country, did Desideri's manuscript become known. Hedin, referring to Desideri's achievements and scholarship, describes him as 'one of the most superb travellers who has ever visited Tibet, and of contemporary travellers the most outstanding and gifted'. Desideri, in fact, was the first European to make a complete circuit of the Himalayas and to give details about the strange, monk-governed state hidden behind the highest mountains of the globe.

In a later volume Hedin returns to the achievement of Desideri:

Desideri's Tibetan geography remains for ever a classic work. It is the first reliable description of Tibet ever given by a European. In topographical detail the lama surveyors who worked at the same time gave much more. But compare Desideri's general morphology, extension and climate of Tibet with the theories of some modern geographers of Rawlinson's time, and you will not hesitate a second as to whom the prize is due.[1]

[1]Sven Hedin, *Southern Tibet* (Stockholm, 1917), vol. 3, 13.

Postscript

The Congregation for the Propagation of the Faith, which had assigned Tibet to the Capuchin friars, had been set up in 1622 as the supreme central governing body of all missionary activity. Its constitution revoked all existing rights, privileges and concessions granted to religious or civil bodies; and it conferred upon the Congregation exclusive judicial authority to settle all disputes concerning the missions.

But it was a long time before the Congregation was able to exercise the powers it had been given. A long-drawn-out struggle ensued and continued into the next century between Propaganda and the so-called Padroado Real or Royal Patronage that the Holy See had granted to Portugal after the discovery of the New World. By the Padroado the Crown of Portugal was granted certain rights over the church in the newly discovered territories, including the appointment of bishops; in return Portugal was to support missionary activity in those lands. The Crown assumed the expenses of training the clergy and conveying them overseas and contributed to their maintenance on the missions.

It was with the cooperation and blessing of the Portuguese viceroy of India that Bento de Goes set out in search of Cathay; and under the same patronage Antonio de Andrade penetrated beyond the northern frontiers of India into Tibet. But it was in China at the time of Grueber's arrival in Peking that the conflict between the Jesuits and Propaganda had dire effects upon the future of the China Mission.

When Matteo Ricci died in Peking in 1610, nine of the eighteen Jesuits in China were Chinese. 'I leave you an open door' were among his last words to his companions. Ricci had carefully examined certain practices of the country, later known collectively as the 'Chinese Rites', and had found nothing in them incompatible with Christian doctrine: chief among them were the ceremonies practised in honour of Confucius, the cult of the family dead, and the use of the Chinese words for heaven and for God (the Supreme Lord and Ruler).

Although Ricci was not without critics in his lifetime, six years after his death Pope Paul V granted the Jesuits permission to use Chinese in the celebration of the Mass, the administration of the sacraments and the recitation of the breviary. But since there was no translation of the Bible then available, some of these privileges could not be used immediately.

The rapid progress of Christianity in China in the years following Ricci's death was halted abruptly when Dominican missionaries arrived from the Philippines under the leadership of Friar Juan Morales, who aroused the hostility of the Chinese by his preaching in public places. Exiled by the Emperor to Macao, Morales went on to Rome, where with the backing of Propaganda he obtained from Innocent X in 1645 a decree condemning the missionary methods of the Jesuits. With the exception of the General of the Jesuits, who realized that the most effective way of promoting Christianity in China was to send eminent scientists, especially mathematicians, to Peking, there was scarcely a person in Rome at the time who understood that Ricci and his successors had discovered a new world, totally different in culture from the West, and that the Jesuits were seeking to bring it into a friendly relationship with Europe.

On his return to China Morales promulgated the decree condemning the Chinese Rites. Appealing to Rome, the Jesuits sent Martino Martini to put their case before the Pope, Alexander VII: Martini had already established a reputation in Europe as the leading Sinologist of the day, thanks to his numerous books on the history and geography of the country. Martini succeeded in persuading the Pope to reverse the decree; in the course of this same visit, he recruited Johannes Grueber and Albert d'Orville for the Chinese Mission.

Opposition to the Jesuits, however, continued. In 1659 Propaganda, exercising its absolute authority over the missions, appointed three vicars apostolic with jurisdiction over the whole of China: all three bishops belonged to the French Foreign Missionary Society, favoured by Propaganda. None had any knowledge of China, none spoke Chinese, yet all had dictatorial jurisdiction over districts that had no administrative existence except on paper. The needs of the Church had been ignored, no advice had been sought and no consultations held.

At the centre of the conflict between the Jesuits and Propaganda was the Jesuit Fr Adam Schall, whose influence with the last Ming emperor made missionary activity possible in the provinces. After the Manchus had thoroughly conquered the empire in 1644, Schall won the favour of the first emperor of the new line, the young Shun-Chih, who embarrassed the Jesuit by raising him to the dignity of a Mandarin of the First Class. It was only after he had refused the dignity three times that the Jesuit was compelled to accept it. At the time of Grueber's arrival in Peking in 1658, Schall had been delated to Rome for practising emperor worship and for observing various superstitious customs, such as genuflecting, in the manner of all mandarins of his degree, on approaching the imperial throne.

Among the papers entrusted to Grueber to take to Rome were three packages (now in the central Jesuit archives in Rome), tightly folded for the convenience of the bearer, each giving a detailed defence of the Jesuit position, the first by Grueber, the second by Schall himself, and the third by Fr Ferdinand Verbiest, the Emperor's astronomer and Schall's collaborator in designing the new calendar.

It now became still more urgent, if the Chinese Mission was to be saved, to find a shorter and safer route for communicating with Rome: the entire future of Christianity in China appeared to depend on the success of Grueber's mission. This perhaps explains why he did not bother to enter into a long description of his epic journey. In fact, only a short time after the departure of Grueber and d'Orville from Peking in 1661, the untimely death of the young Manchu emperor, Shun-Chih, ushered in an anti-Christian reaction under the rule of the regents. Schall, now an old man, was imprisoned in 1664, condemned to death, and later reprieved. He was later totally rehabilitated when the new emperor, a young man named K'ang-Hsi, took over from the regency; he was to rule for the next sixty years. Thanks to Schall's successors, especially Fr Jean-François Gerbillon, who helped to conclude the treaty that determined the frontier between China and Russia, the Jesuits succeeded in re-establishing their influence at court.

Opposition from Propaganda continued. In 1693 the vicars apostolic succeeded in gaining a fresh condemnation of the Chinese Rites. The Jesuits responded by obtaining from Emperor K'ang-Hsi a statement, dated 30 November 1700, endorsing Ricci's interpretation of their customs: the Emperor declared categorically that there was nothing whatever in their traditional practices that had any doctrinal significance. This won a respite for the Jesuits, but only until 1742, when Benedict XIV came down firmly on the side of Propaganda.

It can only be a matter of speculation what success Desideri might have had in Tibet if Propaganda, which was now exercising its authority more effectively, had not been determined to make the country the exclusive missionary preserve of the Capuchin Fathers to the explicit exclusion of the Jesuits. For five years Desideri had made the same intensive study of native customs and beliefs as Ricci had done among the Chinese. There is no record of his having made a single Christian convert. But at the same time he believed that, given a short time longer in Lhasa, the country would have been receptive to Christian teaching. His greatest sadness was the absence of anyone among the Capuchins ready or able to continue his work. While both Desideri and his travelling companion, Fr Freyre, could find no words sufficient to praise the friars for the way they 'skillfully and lovingly' nursed them when on their return to India first Freyre and then Desideri fell gravely sick, yet neither could avoid censuring them severely for their missionary methods. The catechism they proposed to use, authorized by Propaganda and approved by the Pope, was replete with errors owing to the way it had been literally translated. Desideri protested that he would require a whole book to correct them all. 'This is not surprising,' Desideri wrote, 'for instead of learning the language, they [the friars] spent their time in Lhasa distributing medicines.' Moreover, as he was to point out later, it was only in 1727, six years after he had left Tibet, that the first two Capuchins, Fr Orazio della Pena and Fr Felice da Moro, began to study the language, the first seriously, the second hardly at all.

This in itself was proof enough that they had little understanding of the esteem in which Desideri was held among the doctors of the universities or any appreciation of his familiarity with the Tibetan books. They knew nothing, Desideri regretted, of the subtlety of the Tibetan mind, the intricacy of their beliefs, their abstruse errors or their rigorous methods of conducting an argument. But what distressed Desideri most was the failure of the Capuchins to understand the genuine keenness of the Tibetans to get at the truth in their discussions. 'They were most eager,' he insisted, 'to rid themselves of false notions of God and to read my books.'

On his return to Rome, Desideri found Propaganda impervious to any plea: its constitution authorized the Congregation to settle all disputes concerning the missions. Again he appealed to the Pope as he had done from Kuti: his audience with Clement XI had taken place in the company of the Jesuit General's delegate for Italy. He argued that the Pope would never at that time have authorized him to reopen the Jesuit mission in Tibet if Propaganda had allotted the country to the friars as their exclusive preserve. Pope Clement had died in 1721. Nothing came of his appeal.

Whether Desideri had left 'an open door' for his brethren to enter Tibet is again a matter of speculation. Certainly he had no hesitation in claiming that he had 'a well-founded hope of a rich harvest in the future'.

It was not until 1908 that Pope Pius X drew up a new constitution for Propaganda that restricted its competence, abolished its judicial powers, and at the same time did away with the Padroado Real. In 1936 Pius XI rescinded the decree of Benedict XIV condemning the Chinese Rites.

Sources

The principal sources of this book, some of which are already in print, are to be found in the central Jesuit archives in Rome (Borgo S. Spirito, 4). When in the course of this book I supply no page references for quotations from the letters of the Jesuit travellers, the reader can safely assume that the original manuscripts are to be found in the Roman archives of the Society of Jesus and that the translation is my own. Fr Antonio de Andrade's account of his 'discovery' of Tibet was printed first in Lisbon in 1626 under the title *Novo Descobrimento de Gram Cathayo ou Reinos de Tibet*. Of the numerous editions of the book, I have used the Latin, which follows most closely Andrade's original manuscript. Azevedo's account of his travels, *De Agra pera o Tibet*, has been printed in the original Portuguese in C. Wessells's *Early Jesuit Travellers in Central Asia*, Appendix 1, 283–313. It is followed there in Appendix 3 (313–32) by Cacella's journal entitled *Relacão . . . da sua Viagem*, and by a much shorter report on the same journey by Cacella's companion, João Cabral (333–36). For Grueber there are virtually no primary sources apart from a few letters in the Jesuit archives. There is no shortage of material for Desideri. All his writings, including his letters to Propaganda, have been published in three volumes by Luciano Petech in his *I missionari italiani nel Tibet* (Istituto Poligrafico dello Stato, 1954–56). These volumes contain twenty-five letters written by Desideri to Pope Clement XI, Propaganda, and the Jesuit General; an account of his journey to Lhasa; a description of the climate, customs, civil government and religion of Tibet; a narrative of his departure from Lhasa and his return via Katmandu and Patna to Europe; and summaries (amounting in all to some seventy large printed pages) of his defence against criticisms of his conduct by the Capuchin Fr Felice de Montevecchio and others. Further sources for Desideri and others are listed in the Bibliography.

Bibliography

Bernard, H. *Le frère Bento de Goes chez les Musulmans de la Haute Asie, 1603–1607*. Tientsin, 1934.

Bosmans, H. *Documents sur Albert Dorville*. Bureaux des Analectes, Louvain, 1911.

Brill, E. J. *Cinq lettres du Père Gerbillon*. Leiden, 1906.

Cable, C. M., and F. French. *The Gobi Desert*. London, 1950.

Castellani, O., S.J. 'Il Padre Ippolyte Desideri e sua missione nel Tibet, 1684–1733.' *Civiltà Cattolica*, 1934, 115ff.

Cronin, Vincent. *The Wise Man from the West*. London, 1955.

Dawson, Christopher, ed. *The Mission to Asia: Narratives and Letters of the Franciscan Missionaries in Mongolia and China in the Thirteenth and Fourteenth Centuries*. London, 1955.

Fleming, Peter. *Bayonets to Lhasa*. London, 1961.

———. *Travels in Tartary*, London, 1936.

French, Patrick. *Younghusband, The Last Great Imperial Adventurer*. London, 1994.

Guerreiro, Fernão, S.J. *Jahangir and the Jesuits*. London, 1930.

Harrer, Heinrich. *Seven Years in Tibet*. London, 1953.

Hedin, Sven. *Southern Tibet: Discoveries in Former Times Compared with My Own Researches*. 4 vols. Stockholm, 1917.

Heras, H., S.J. 'The Tomb of Fr Albert D'Orville, S.J.' *Archivum Historicum S. I.* 2 (1933): 17–24.

Hopkirk, Peter. *Trespassers on the Roof of the World*. Oxford, 1986.

Huc, Régis-Evariste. *Lamas of the Western Heaven*. Trans. Charles de Salis. The Folio Society, 1982.

———. *Travels in Tartary, Tibet, and China during the Years 1844–1846*. London, 1856.

Jann, Adelhelm, O. Min. Cap. *Die katholischen Missionen in Indien, China, und Japan*. Paderborn, 1915.

Jarric, Pierre du, S.J. *Akbar and the Jesuits*. London, 1926.

Kircher, Athanasius. *China Illustrata*. Amsterdam, 1667.

Montserrate, A. *The Commentary of Fr Montserrate, S.J., on His Journey to the Court of Akbar*. Oxford, 1922.

Petech, Luciano. *I missionarii italiani nel Tibet*. Part 4. Rome, 1953.

Polo, Marco. *The Travels of Marco Polo*. Penguin Books, 1958.

Rauty, Natale. 'Notizie inedite sur Hippolite Desideri e sulla sua familia tratte dagli archivi Pistoiesi.' Pistoia, 1984.

Ryder, Major C. S. D. 'The Exploration and Survey with the Tibet Frontier Commission, and from Gyangtse to Simla via Gartok.' *Geographical Journal* 26 (October 1905).

Ricci, Matteo, *Opere storiche.* Ed. P. Tacchi Venturi. Macerata, 1911–13.

Thomson, Thomas. *Western Himalaya and Tibet: A Narrative of a Journey through the Mountains of Northern India during the Years 1847–48.* London, 1852.

Toscano, G. M. 'Contributo del Desideri alla conoscenza dell'Asia nel secolo XVIII.' In *La Conoscenza dell'Asia e dell'Africa in Italia nei secoli XVIII e XIX.* Vol. 1. Naples, 1984.

———. *La prima missione cattolica nel Tibet.* Parma: Istituto Missioni Estere, 1951.

Trigault, N., S.J. *De christiana expeditione apud Sinas.* Cologne, 1617.

Waddell, L. A. *Lhasa and Its Mysteries.* London, 1905

Wessells, C. *Early Jesuit Travellers in Central Asia, 1603–1721.* The Hague, 1924.

Wood, John. *A Journey to the Source of the River Oxus.* London, 1872.

Maps

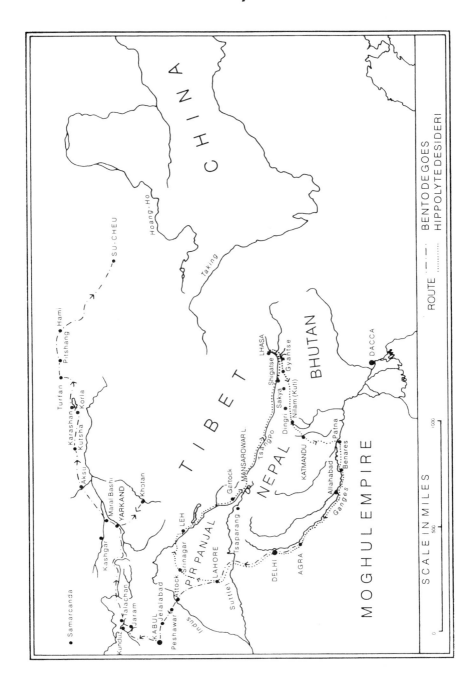

SCALE IN MILES

ROUTE —·—·— BENTO DE GOES

············· HIPPOLYTE DESIDERI

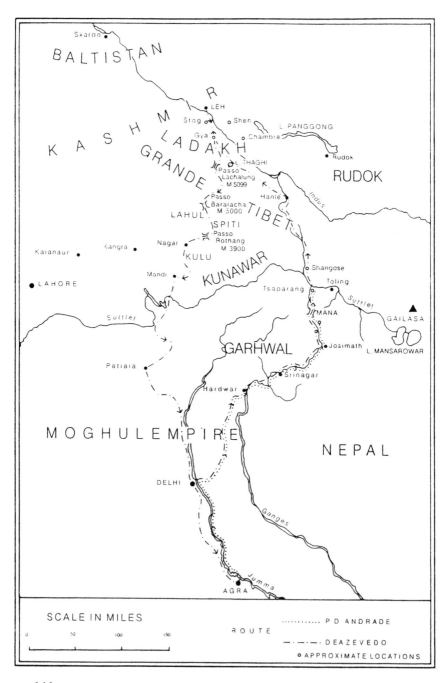

SCALE IN MILES

0   50   100   150

ROUTE

.... P D ANDRADE

—·—·— DE AZEVEDO

○ APPROXIMATE LOCATIONS

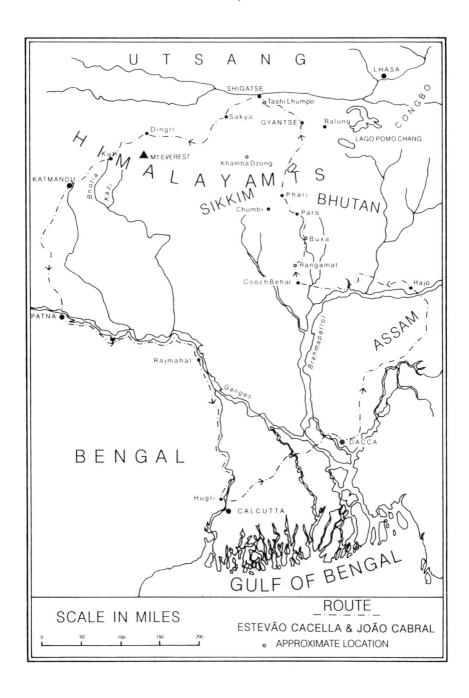

SCALE IN MILES

ROUTE

ESTEVÃO CACELLA & JOÃO CABRAL

o APPROXIMATE LOCATION

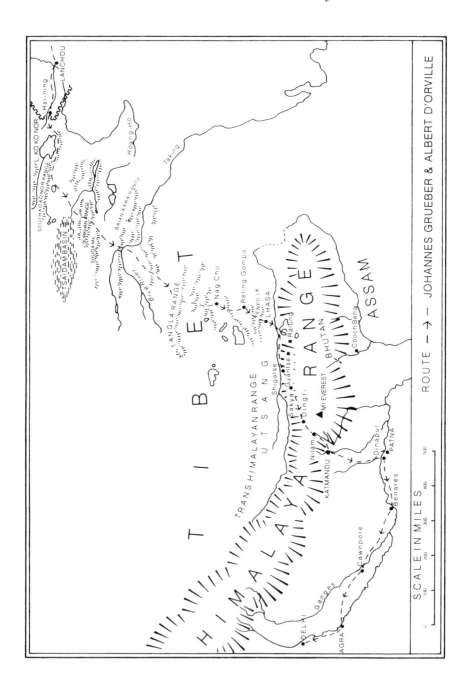

Index

at Surat, 85
in the Tangla Mountains, 95
at Tattah, 103
in the Trans-Himalayan Range, 96
in Tsinghai Province, 90
Guelofs, 71
Guge (Chaparangue), 43, 46, 55, 56
Gushi Khan, 80, 120
Gya, 54
Gyantse, 67, 131
Gylongs, 74

Hamilton, Dr A., 69
Harcourt, A.F.P., 59
Hardwar, 36
Harrer, Heinrich, 61, 97
Hastings, Warren, 69
Hedin, Sven, 48, 89, 102, 107, 136
Himalayas, 5, 20, 34, 45, 57
Hindu Kush Mountains, 6, 17, 18, 19, 20
Hindustan, 5, 11, 36
Hsining (Si-ning), 90, 91, 104, 125
Huc, Abbé Régis-Evariste, 92, 93, 94
Hugli, 64, 80

Indus, 5, 15
Innocent IV, Pope, 2
Innocent X, Pope, 138
Isaac, 14, 30, 31
Isfahan, 84, 85

jade, 24, 25
Jang Reting Gompa monastery, 96
Jellalabad, 16
Jussy, 51

K'ang-Hsi, 139
Kaa-n-ghiur, 122
Kabul, 17
Kafirstan, 17
Kailas (Kang-Rinpoche), 117
Kanjur, 24
Karachi, 103
Kashmir, 37, 44, 111
Katmandu, 78, 100, 101
Kaffir(s), 17
Kerala, 63
Khaa-n-dro-ma, 126
Khorap, 121

Khotan, 24
Khyber Pass, 16
Kiayukwan, 27
Kircher, Fr Athanasius, 82, 83
Koko-Nor, 88, 91, 92, 93
Kublai Khan, 10, 42
Kucha, 26
Kum-Bum, 92
Kuti (Nilam Dzong), 78, 99, 130, 132
Kuyuk Khan, 2

Lachalung, 58
Ladakh, 49, 52, 54, 55, 112
Lahore, 11, 45, 103, 111
Lahul, 57
Lanchow, 90
Leh, 52, 53, 113
Lha-Brang, 120
Lhasa, 74, 76, 80, 96, 115, 119–20
Lhobas, 127
Lho-ro, 127
Liquinarane, 64, 65–6

Macao, 84, 85, 86
Macassar (Ujung Pandang), 89
Malabar, 35
Mana, 40, 41, 52
Mana Pass, 34, 41, 44, 52
Mana Range, 56
Manasarovar, 118
Mandi, 59
Marco Polo, 3, 5, 19, 20, 21, 26, 27, 92
Markham, Clements, 74
Marques, Manuel, 36, 40, 41, 46, 51
Martini, Fr Martino, 89, 138
Messi (Maisi), 134
Mirjudin, 90
Mirza Shahruch, 19
Mont Blanc, 34
Montgomerie, T.G., 7, 99
Montserrate, Antonio de, 15, 16
Moorcroft, William, 57
Moro, Fr Felice da, 140
Mount Kastel, 111, 112
Mount Shuga, 93
Mozambique, 109
Mundus Subterraneus, 82
Mur-Ussa (Blue River), 95
Mysore, 108